MW01268019

Chasing Rainbows

A Search for Family Ties

by Laurel Lynn

To Joe Ann,
Follow your
own rainbow, and
good luck with
always follow you.
Laurel Lynn
1992

Adoption Awareness Press
Division of The Musser Foundation
P.O. Box 1860
Cape Coral, FL 33910

Everything in this book is true. However, to insure privacy, the names and locations have been changed.

Cover Illustration by Mary Dalsing
Olathe, Kansas

ACKNOWLEDGEMENTS

Heartfelt thanks to Hazel Ford, without whose help this book could never have been written.

Sincere thanks to Marshall Cook, who helped and encouraged me.

Thanks to June Tanner for her patient guidance.

Many thanks to Wilma Passler and Terri Hitt for their loyal friendship.

Special thanks to my husband Don and daughter Debbie Basler for their love and support.

Last but not least, a big thank you to the Musser Foundation.

In loving memory of my adoptive parents

Table of Contents

1 Like an Old Shoe............................. 9
2 Just Trust Me................................ 13
3 Disaster in Bronze........................... 19
4 Empty Promises............................... 23
5 Into Exile................................... 27
6 Love and Warm Milk........................... 31
7 Waiting For My Beloved....................... 35
8 A Horrible Nightmare......................... 39
9 Doesn't Anyone Listen?....................... 43
10 Two Outcasts at Christmas.................... 47
11 If Mother Loved Me........................... 51
12 You Can Have Another Baby.................... 55
13 Second Choice................................ 59
14 Against the Rules............................ 63
15 What's Best For Baby......................... 67
16 Sign Here.................................... 71
17 No Decent Man................................ 75
18 Two Needles in a Haystack.................... 79
19 Waiting (Im)patiently........................ 85
20 Say Hello!................................... 89
21 Beautiful & Bittersweet...................... 92
22 It Would Break My Mother's Heart............. 99
23 Call Me Sarah................................ 103
24 Goodbye....Again............................. 107
25 Let's Make A Deal............................ 111
26 Up in Smoke.................................. 115
27 Let This Be It............................... 119
28 Scared to Death.............................. 123
29 For a Lifetime............................... 127
30 A Bond That Goes Beyond...................... 131
31 Many Questions Answered...................... 137
32 My Mother is Your Mother?.................... 141
33 Just Like Sisters........................... 145
34 Rainbow's End................................ 151

1

Like An Old Shoe

Officially my life began at age four months when my parents took me home to live with them as their adopted daughter Sarah. My earliest recollections are living on a farm in a midwestern state where I lived happily with my mother, father, an older brother Frank, and my grandmother whom I loved with all my heart. Although I had always known I was adopted, the word "adopted" meant nothing to me. I was there and didn't worry about how I got there. Life was good.

I cannot remember much about the early years except the wonderful weekends I spent with my father. He would lift me up onto his horse, a Tennessee walking horse who stood seventeen hands high, and we would ride together for what seemed like hours. During the week, he was gone. He left the house before I awoke in the morning and didn't return until after I had gone to sleep at night. When I inquired about his whereabouts, Grandmother said, "We're living in a depression. Times are bad. Your father works late so that he can provide well for his family."

Our farm was a working farm. A hired man named Randy milked the cows, fed the stock and tended to the fields. Randy's wife Rachel did the washing and ironing, cooked the meals and kept the house clean. Very little is stored in my memory about my mother. She was busy with her social, church and civic organizations. My grandmother, who lived with us for as long as I could recall, was my constant companion. Many times she read me story after story until her voice became hoarse. My favorites were Billy Whiskers and Grimm's Fairy Tales that I remember to this day.

My brother Frank, as far as I was concerned, had no faults. I adored him, and the times we spent together are happy times to remember. We played games, sang songs and when I was old enough, we rode horseback together. We would race Frank's high-spirited Morgan mare and my cantankerous, stubborn Shetland pony over the open fields and back to the barn. It didn't worry me that Frank was not biologically related to me; he was my brother, and that's all that mattered.

When I was five years old, my life changed. My father, a certified life underwriter for a large insurance company, was transferred. Our family, along with three registered saddle horses (I had outgrown my pony and she was sold), a large collie, a German shepherd, and two Siamese cats, moved to a city near Boston, Massachusetts. Because I was a shy, timid child, it was difficult for me to start a new school, especially since it was the middle of the term. Immediately, the other children made fun of me; they thought I had a funny-sounding western accent.

Although our new home was located in the country on five acres, it was not a farm. We lived in a beautiful, large two-story house, but I missed the carefree life I had known on the farm.

Mother was too busy to spend time with me. Dad was gone most of the time. His job required him to travel extensively. My brother was in high school and didn't have time for his little sister. Randy and Rachael did not move with us, but a woman my mother referred to as my governess, Miss Cheesebrough, did. I couldn't pronounce her name, so I called her Aunt Carry. I didn't like Aunt Carry. To get away from her, I insisted my grandmother saddle my new Welsh pony named Duchess, so that I could ride miles from home to escape into a wonderful secret world of my own. Because no one in my family seemed to have time for me, I was lonesome and unhappy.

One day Mother announced we were moving back to the midwest. She explained that because of Dad's travels, he was never home when my brother came home from college. Also, Dad complained that every time he returned from a business trip, I had grown a foot. Mother said that although she didn't want to leave her friends - we had lived there five years - she was excited about moving to a city where one of her sisters lived. "Sarah, you'll have cousins there," she told me. I was not impressed.

Mother and Grandmother stayed behind to close up the house while Dad and I drove to what would be our new home. When we reached our destination, Dad dropped me off at my aunt's house. He kissed me on the cheek, told me he would be living in a hotel near his office, and then he turned and left.

There I was with an aunt, uncle and three cousins I didn't even know. Without my mother and grandmother, there was no home. Every night when I went to bed in a small room that I shared with two of my cousins, I turned my face to the wall and cried. Although my cousins, Jeanne, Lillian, and Martha, were nice to me, they had lives of their own and didn't have time for me. I felt like a misfit.

When Mother and Grandmother finally came, my life returned to normal; at least we were a family under the same roof. This time we moved into a large, colonial house in town. We stabled the horses out in the country at an exclusive riding club. The two dogs lived with us, but Mother wouldn't allow them into the house. "Dogs belong in the country," she said, threatening to get rid of them. Grandmother came to my rescue: "Sarah loves the dogs. It would break her heart if you got rid of them." The dogs stayed.

My cousin Jeanne, who was about my age, and I had become friends. One afternoon, we were in my bedroom talking, laughing and trying on make-up. Suddenly, Jeanne looked at me and stared into my face.

"You're not my real cousin," she blurted out.

"What are you talking about?" I asked, puzzled.

"Well, you don't belong to this family."

"Yes, I do."

"No, you don't. You're adopted."

"I know, but what difference does it make?"

"It makes all the difference in the world. Because you're adopted, you're not related to me. You don't belong, and...."

Before Jeanne could say another word, I stood and placed my hands firmly on my hips. Then I yelled, "I belong just as much as you do. My parents picked me out. I'm special. You're just green with envy because my mother and father went to a lot of trouble to get me."

"Well," said Jeanne, "your real mother didn't want you. She threw you away like an old shoe. Then you became an orphan. My best friend told me that your real mother probably wasn't married. And there's a name for people like you: bastard. You're a bastard! You don't belong here."

"Yes, I do," I said, indignantly.

"No, you don't belong anywhere."

"I hate you," I screamed. "You're a horrible girl."

Losing control, I shoved Jeanne out of my room and slammed the door in her face. I felt as though someone had kicked me in the pit of my stomach, and knew I would never, ever forget what my cousin had said to me that day.

Later when I told my mother about it, she shrugged. "Sarah," she said, "you shouldn't pay any attention to the cruel words of a little girl who doesn't know any better."

A chill ran through me. Jeanne's words had crushed me. I wanted my mother to take me into her arms and hold me - to tell me that I did, indeed, belong to the family. But she walked away, leaving me alone, staring after her.

That night, tears soaked my pillow.

2

Just Trust Me

I n the spring of 1948, having skipped two grades in elementary school, I graduated from a private girls' high school. Although I was just sixteen years old, my parents enrolled me in a college that was an elite, expensive, private school for young women. I had been told by my mother it was a difficult college to get into, since it was small and accepted only a select few.

During my teenage years, my mother and I did not get along well. That prompted me to think often about my real mother. There was a feeling of loneliness inside me which I couldn't explain even to myself. In spite of the comforts and luxuries provided me by my parents, there was something significant missing in my life – my identity! I was curious about myself and wondered who I was and where I had come from. I knew someday I would search for my biological mother. I thought about her a lot, especially when I was angry with my parents.

Then my priorities changed – I met Mike. I fell for him like a ton of bricks.

When I introduced him to my parents, I sensed immediately they didn't approve of him. However, that didn't surprise me. They rarely liked anyone I dated. I resented their criticism of my friends and thought it was degrading. Despite the constant arguments and fervent protests, particularly from my mother, I continued to go out with Mike. This, of course, led to more friction between my mother and me. She reiterated often that Mike was too old for me. But I loved him and believed my life had never been happier.

It wasn't long until I started to drink beer, smoke cigarettes and, in time, submit to Mike's lovemaking. He made me feel special. He made me feel loved. When he and I were together, I forgot about my parents and their strict rules. More importantly, I forgot about being adopted.

It had been drilled into my head since childhood that a respectable young woman from a good home should remain a virgin until she married. But I was convinced Mike would marry me, so why wait? As the summer months neared an end, my brother Frank and his wife Linda came home for a visit. The house was full of laughter and sunshine for everyone except me. There was no doubt in my mind that I was pregnant.

Worried and confused, I needed time alone to think. Consequently, I stayed in my bedroom and hid from my family. I thought about the past and how much I had missed my brother when he had left home to start college. When Pearl Harbor had been attacked by Japan in 1941, Frank joined the Naval Air Corps, and when the war was over, he returned to Yale University to complete his education. Then he married and started a life of his own. Prior to his marriage, I had him all to myself, but when he married Linda, I was forced to share him. Believing the special relationship between the two of us would never, ever be the same, I was unhappy. While thinking fondly about my brother, I contemplated telling him that I was pregnant, but quickly changed my mind. Frank, who was a lot like Mother, just wouldn't understand.

Initially, I had been excited about going away to school. I looked forward to the day I would be on my own and out from under my mother's watchful, eagle eye. But after I met Mike and fell in love with him, college no longer interested me. Now, knowing I was going to have a baby, I also knew my plans would change. How could I start college knowing I was pregnant?

It wasn't long until Frank noticed I was withdrawn and moody. When he confronted me concerning my lack of enthusiasm about starting a wonderful new life as a college student, I sarcastically told him to mind his own business. Then I added, hastily, "Oh, don't pay any attention to me. I'm just tired, I guess. Mother's been running me ragged taking me shopping almost every day for what she considers an appropriate college wardrobe." Forcing a smile to avoid further conversation and questions, I ran upstairs to my bedroom where my thoughts turned to Mike.

Since I was scheduled to leave for school in the very near future, I knew I couldn't put off telling Mike I was expecting his baby. I shivered at the thought of what he would say. No matter how hard I tried, I couldn't escape reality. Fear grabbed me.

That evening, knowing I couldn't put off the inevitable, I told Mike I was pregnant.

"You're what?" he screamed.

"You heard me - I'm expecting your baby."

"Sarah, are you sure?"

"I'm positive."

"Oh, my God. Oh, my God!"

After numerous emotional discussions between Mike and me, we decided the only logical thing to do was marry. Mike suggested I arrange a luncheon between us and my parents so that he could ask them for their permission. "Trust me," he said. "Trust me and everything will work out fine."

My mother was a strict disciplinarian who set all the rules and regulations around which my family's lives revolved. I was apprehensive about asking if she and Dad would have lunch with us. Regardless, after much persuasion on my part, she reluctantly agreed to have lunch with us the following Friday.

Meanwhile, my active imagination became even more active. Convinced my parents would look at me and know I was pregnant, I stayed away from them. Impatiently, I waited for Friday even though I thought it was a waste of time. I knew my parents neither approved of Mike nor liked him. Once or twice, I thought about telling Mother I was pregnant, but I was afraid of her and changed my mind. I truly believed with all my heart, since I was her adopted daughter, if she knew I was expecting a baby, she would disown me. Terribly distraught and constantly worried, I wondered why something as beautiful and pure as my love for Mike had turned ugly and sour.

When Friday came, Mike picked me up and we drove downtown together. We were to meet my parents at my father's businessmen's club at precisely one o'clock. Knowing Dad was adamant about punctuality, I wanted to get there on time. But when we arrived at the club, my parents were waiting for us.

Mike shook hands with my father and politely greeted my mother.

The maitre d' ushered us to a table located in the center of the crowded dining room. When he seated us, I felt conspicuous. I was uncomfortable and believed everyone in the dining room was staring directly at me.

The conversation among the four of us was trivial and trite. I didn't want to discuss the weather; I wanted Mike to ask my parents what he had come here to ask them. When he didn't, I glared into his face, defiantly.

Mike cleared his throat. He straightened his tie. Then, reaching across the table, he took my hand in his and blurted out, "I love your daughter. I respectfully ask for your permission to marry Sarah."

There was dead silence.

I held my breath.

Suddenly Mother started talking loudly and I felt as if all eyes were on me. I was forced to sit there and listen as she verbalized her disapproval of Mike's marriage proposal.

"Sarah," she said, angrily, "you're far too young to even entertain the thought of marriage. You evidently don't appreciate the opportunity your father and I have given you by sending you to one of the very best colleges available. You have been given a chance for a good education that is denied most young women."

I opened my mouth to interrupt, but my mother gestured me quiet.

She continued to lecture me while my father echoed her every word. The waiter served our lunch. I reached for a glass of water and accidentally spilled it. Water went everywhere, soaking the tablecloth and drip-

ping down onto Mike's lap. Chagrined, I stood up, threw my napkin
down and ran off, leaving Mike sitting alone with my irate parents.
Without a backward glance, I ran out of the club and onto the busy
sidewalk, where I was swallowed by a crowd of shoppers. I wandered
around for hours, and when it started to get dark, I took a bus home.
When I got there, I ran upstairs to my bedroom and slammed the
door. A short time later, I heard someone knocking. I ignored it, but the
knocking persisted.
"Go away," I yelled. "Just go away and leave me alone."
Without any invitation to enter my room, Hettie, who had been em-
ployed by my family for many years, walked in. When I looked up, I saw
she was carrying a dinner tray.
"Miss Sarah," she said, "I'm worried about you. You haven't been
yourself lately." Without another word, she put the tray on the night
stand and quickly left the room.
The poignant aroma of roast beef, mashed potatoes dripping with
rich brown gravy reached my nostrils. Hungry and tired, I devoured every bite; then I closed my eyes and welcomed sleep.
When I awoke the next morning, I stayed in my room to avoid conversation or possible arguments with my parents. Impatiently, I paced
the floor and waited for a telephone call from Mike. But he didn't call.
Finally, angry and upset, I telephoned him.
"Why haven't you called me?" I asked.
"Because I have nothing to say to you."
"Well, I said, "I have plenty to say to you."
That afternoon, we met in the park, in the beautiful rose garden,
near my house. He was furious with me for having left him sitting alone
with my parents. His gentle blue eyes were cold and distant-looking. I
sensed he was different somehow. He acted weird – like a stranger.
When I reached for his hand, he pulled away. His mood frightened me. I
didn't know what to do or what to say. Finally, close to tears, I whispered, "Mike, we just have to get married right away."
"We can't. You're too young to get married without parental permission. And if we ran off and got married, your parents would have the
marriage annulled. Or have you changed your mind and decided to tell
them you're pregnant?"
"No, of course not. If they knew, they probably would want me to
have an abortion."
"Perhaps you should consider an abortion."
"Never! I want my baby. Don't you understand? I'm not related to
anyone. I don't even know what it feels like to be related to someone.
But I'll be truly related to my baby. Abortion? Never!"
"Well, Sarah, if you feel that strongly about it, your only alternative
is to start college as planned."
"How can I start school knowing I can't stay?"
"No one knows about your pregnancy except you and me."
"But, Mike...."
"Just go on down to school and act as if nothing is wrong. I'll see you

16

every weekend. And after I've had a chance to work things out, we'll get married."

"Promise?"

"Yes, don't worry. Trust me and everything will work out. Just trust me."

3

Disaster in Bronze

Three days later, I was ready to leave for college. I remember what should have been one of the happiest days in my life was one of the saddest. I had trouble coping, for I knew I was leaving what for years had been my comfort zone. I believed it was a mistake to start college, but I didn't know what else to do.

"Sarah, don't dawdle," my mother called out. "Your father's been waiting over an hour to drive you to school."

"I'm coming, Mother," I answered, hastily. When I kissed her and my grandmother goodbye, I glanced at my familiar surroundings as if I were seeing my home for the last time. I wanted to say to my mother, "I can't go; I'm pregnant." Instead, I got into the car with my father.

About an hour and a half later we arrived at school. I met my roommate, Gloria, for the first time. After the introductions were over and my luggage had been taken to my dormitory room, Dad leaned over and kissed my forehead. "Be a good girl," he said. "And make good grades."

He turned, waved, and got back into his car. As I watched him drive away, my heart sank. I knew my life as a college student had begun.

Under normal circumstances, I'm certain I would have liked college life, but I was miserable. I imagined all the other girls looked at me and knew I was pregnant. Consequently, I kept to myself, making it difficult to make new friends.

After several weeks had passed and I still had not heard from Mike, I started to panic. He hadn't come to see me, nor had he written or called as promised. I had written to him many times, but had not received a reply. For years, I had believed that my real mother had deserted me. Now I believed Mike had deserted me, too. My spirits plummeted.

No matter how bad I felt, I still had to participate in all the school social activities. One was the faculty tea in Lowell Hall. Although my

19

mother had provided me with a closet-full of dresses, I didn't like any of them. We had never shared the same taste in clothes. Not knowing what to wear to the tea, I decided to go into town to one of the large department stores and charge a new dress to Mother's account. When I got to the store, I looked at all the available dresses. Then a sales clerk, a pleasant-looking woman with a friendly smile, asked me if I needed any help. "Yes," I said, "I'm looking for something nice to wear to a faculty tea."

"I have exactly what you're looking for," the clerk answered as she took a blue chiffon dress from the rack and held it up for me to admire. "With your beautiful dark hair and large hazel eyes, you'll look lovely in this one..."

"No," I interrupted. "I don't like it. I already have three blue dresses. I'm looking for something in bronze satin. Bronze is in this year."

"My dear," said the clerk, "bronze would do nothing for you. It's not your color."

"But I want a bronze satin dress," I repeated, impatiently.

"Whatever you say," the clerk said as she took a bronze satin dress down from the rack.

"That's the one I want. I'll take it."

"Don't you want to try it on?"

"No, if it's a size nine, it will fit me."

Without arguing, the clerk nodded and asked me to step over to the cash register. Pleased with my purchase, I signed my mother's name to the sales slip. I walked back to school with a smile on my face and the dress box tucked securely under my arm. When I got to my room, I proudly showed Gloria my new dress.

"It's pretty," she said. Then she added nonchalantly that she wasn't sure it was my color. By the time she had finished talking, I had put on the dress and was standing in front of the full-length mirror.

"You're right. I hate it," I said. "The bronze color against my olive complexion makes me look anemic. And it's too small. It makes me look fat." Scowling, I stared at the dress and saw that the satin clung tightly to my body, revealing my every curve. "I should have listened to the sales clerk," I mumbled as I took off the dress and carelessly threw it down on the floor.

Gloria stooped down and picked up the dress. She held it at arm's length. "It's a beautiful dress and..."

"Do you want to wear it?

"Yes, I'd love to. Thanks."

That afternoon, I wore a pale blue chiffon dress, which Mother had provided for me. When the faculty tea was over, Gloria returned the bronze satin dress which I hung up in my closet. I knew I would never wear it.

Two days later, Mother appeared at school in a huff. She was angry with me for charging a new dress to her account without asking permission. She insisted that I accompany her to the department store, and escorted me to the dress department.

"Do you see this girl?" she asked the sales clerk.

"Yes, Ma'am. I sold her a dress a couple of days ago. Is there something wrong?"

"Yes, there's something wrong. I want you to take a good look at her and don't let her charge anything to my account ever again."

I felt the blood rushing to my head. I imagined my face had turned crimson with shame. I was mortified. For the moment, I hated my mother. Without a word, I turned and ran out of the store to the car. When Mother joined me, I was forced to listen as she went on and on about the dress.

"Young lady," she said. "You should have known better than to charge a new dress to my account. You're spoiled, Sarah. You have more dresses than any girl I know, yet you bought another one. Honestly, I just don't understand you. I want you to pay me back every penny from the allowance your father gives you. Do you hear me?"

"Yes, Mother."

"Well, I hope you have learned a lesson. And, for your sake, I hope you will never do such a foolish, irresponsible thing again."

"No, Mother, I won't."

The minute we got back to school, I got out of the car without a backward glance. Mother drove off with such momentum it slammed the car door. I ran to my dormitory room and telephoned my father to tell him what had happened. I needed a kind word.

After listening patiently, Dad said, "Sarah, calm yourself. I'm sorry if your mother embarrassed you, but you should have asked her permission before purchasing a new dress."

"But, Dad, if I had asked her, she would have said no. Sometimes I think Mother hates me."

"No, Sarah, your mother doesn't hate you. She loves you. She wants you to grow up to be a responsible woman who knows the difference between right and wrong. What you did, my dear, was wrong."

"Well, maybe....but, Dad, Mother wants me to pay her back for the dress. I don't have enough money."

"Don't worry, dear," said my father. "I'll send you what you need to repay your mother. But you must promise not to tell her that I sent you the extra money. If you do, it will make matters worse."

"No, Dad, I won't tell Mother. I promise."

4

Empty Promises

My recollections of the days that followed are as vivid as they are painful. Unhappy and frightened, I lost all hope of seeing Mike again. Many times I was tempted to give way to hysteria, believing that my life was ruined. Often I wished I had a sympathetic friend to talk to. Suffering frequent backaches, I thought about going to the nurse's office, but feared the school nurse would suspect I was pregnant. Although I knew I couldn't stay in school, I didn't want to risk getting kicked out. Nervous and irritable, I envied the other girls who acted as if they were happy and carefree.

One morning as I stepped out of the shower, I stood in front of the mirror and viewed my naked body. I noticed I had gained weight. My waistline had thickened and my breasts were enlarged. My nipples were swollen and dark. As if to hide from myself, I grabbed a robe. Although I wanted to cry, the tears were buried too deep.

The weekends were the most miserable times of all. While the other girls were busy making plans with their boyfriends, I was sinking deeper and deeper into depression. Why me, I wondered?

One Friday evening the dormitory was buzzing with excitement and lively chatter of happy students. The bell rang for me to go downstairs to greet a guest. Thinking it was my parents, I wasn't overjoyed. Slowly, I walked down the long, circular staircase. Halfway down, I stopped in mid-step. There he was, handsome and tall, looking up at me! Excitedly, I rushed into Mike's arms and smothered him with hugs and kisses. I wanted to hate him for having tortured me with his absence, but I loved him too much.

Mike stepped back and removed my arms from around his neck. Acting embarrassed, he took me aside and whispered, "Sarah, please don't kiss me like that in front of all these girls."

Nodding, I asked him if he would wait for me while I ran back upstairs to change my clothes.

He said he would.

"I'll only be a minute," I mouthed over my shoulder as I took the steps two at a time. When I got to my room, Gloria was busy getting ready for her date. When she saw me, she asked, "Why are you all smiles?"

"Because Mike's here," I said, as I fastened my garter belt and pulled on my stockings. I nearly fell over backward when I tried to straighten the seams. When I finished dressing, I checked my makeup, ran a brush through my hair and put fresh perfume behind my ears. Straightening my seams again, I ran downstairs expecting to see Mike. But he wasn't there.

"If you're looking for your boyfriend," one of the girls said, "he went outside."

I ran out the front door in search of him. I was relieved to find him sitting on the dormitory steps, where he was smoking a cigarette.

"I thought maybe you had left," I said.

"No, I'm still here. It's just that I didn't want to wait inside with all those college girls staring at me."

We walked to a park bench on campus and sat down. It was against the rules for the girls to ride in cars - a rule often broken - but since I wanted to talk to Mike, I thought the park bench was as good a place as any. Sitting close to him, my heart pounded.

"I'm glad you're here," I murmured. "I knew you'd come for me. Now we can get married..."

"No, Sarah, that's not the reason I came."

"Have you forgotten I'm expecting your baby?"

"How could I forget? It's just that...."

Losing my temper, I stood up and announced loudly, "I'm beginning to show. It won't be long until everyone knows I'm pregnant. I'll get kicked out of school."

"You don't show yet. Do you enjoy worrying about nothing?" As he spoke, the veins in Mike's neck stood out. He looked away. He refused to make eye contact with me.

"If you didn't come to get me, why did you come?"

"There's something I want to tell you."

"I'm sick of listening to you. I'm tired of waiting around for you, and I'm fed up with all your phony, empty promises. I knew it was a mistake for me to start school. If you don't agree to marry me at once, I'll write to my brother Frank and tell him everything."

"What do you think you'll accomplish by writing to your brother?" Don't be dumb, Sarah. Don't you understand? You're still underage."

"Why didn't you think about my age before you got me pregnant?"

"Oh, how I wish I had."

"You told me to trust you. You told me everything would work out all right. You lied. My life's a mess, and all because of you. I hate you! I never want to see you again!"

24

As I ran faster and farther away from him, I heard Mike calling my name. I kept running until I reached my dormitory room, slammed the door, and collapsed onto my bed. An hour or so later, Gloria came in from her date, and I was still lying there crying.

"What's wrong?" she asked.

"I can't tell you."

"Yes, you can. We're roommates. You can tell me anything."

"I broke up with Mike."

"Is that all? For a minute I thought maybe you were sick."

"I am sick."

"Don't worry. I'm sure you'll feel better soon. If you ask me, it's about time you broke up with him. All you've done since school started is make yourself miserable worrying about Mike. Believe me, no man's worth it."

Shrugging, I walked to the window, rested my elbows on the sill, and stared at the stars in the darkening sky. I felt numb. Unaware of the emotional stress I was suffering, Gloria kept talking.

"You've been missing out on a lot of fun by going with one guy. Now you can go out with..."

Abruptly I turned and faced her. "You don't understand," I said. "I'm pregnant with Mike's baby."

"Oh, Sarah! I knew you were upset about something, but I never dreamed you were pregnant! Why didn't you tell me?"

"I was tempted to tell you. There were times when I thought I'd explode if I didn't talk to someone, but I was afraid you'd think badly of me."

"I'd never think badly of a person just because she made a mistake."

"My pregnancy's not a mistake. I love Mike."

"Why didn't he marry you before you started college?"

"It's a long story."

"Do your parents know you're pregnant?"

"No, I couldn't tell them."

"Maybe you should reconsider."

"I just can't tell my parents. The only one I can tell is my brother. That's what Mike and I were arguing about. When I threatened to write to Frank, Mike got furious. I lost my temper, told him I hated him and ran away. Oh, Lord, what have I done? What am I going to do now?"

"Well, if I were you," said Gloria, "I'd write that letter to my brother."

Hours later when I looked down, I saw scraps of paper crumpled all over the floor where I had thrown them. One blank piece of paper lay on my desk. Leaning back in the chair, I stared at the ceiling. I was sick. I had a throbbing headache. My stomach hurt, and my heart pounded in my chest. Finally, after agonizing over every word I wrote, I finished the most difficult letter I had ever written in my entire life. I opened the desk drawer and found a stamp. I placed it firmly on the carefully addressed envelope.

I threw a sweater over my shoulders, left my dormitory room, and walked outside to find a mailbox. Off in a distance, I heard the muffled, lonesome whistle of a train. Fallen autumn leaves crunched under my feet. When I reached the campus mailbox, I shivered in the cold night air.

Hesitating a long moment, I slowly opened the mailbox and dropped the letter inside. I reopened the mailbox once to make certain the letter was gone. It was gone; the mailbox had swallowed my cry for help.

5

Into Exile

I slept late Saturday morning and awoke with a start. I had been dreaming about Mike. I imagined I could smell the masculine aroma of his aftershave lotion. I could feel the strength of his arms around me and the presence of his warm lips on mine. When I suddenly remembered that I had left Mike sitting on the park bench the night before, I broke out in a cold sweat. As I sat on the edge of the bed, I stared at the floor and twisted my hair. "Why did I let my temper get the better of me?" I asked myself.

Gloria, already showered and dressed, seemed to catch the essence of my mood.

"How do you feel?" she asked, thoughtfully.

"I feel awful."

"I'm sorry. I wish there was something I could do or say to help you."

"You've been a big help. Just having someone to talk to has been wonderful."

"Well, I'm glad you wrote to your brother."

"I didn't know what else to do."

Graciously extending a hand in friendship, Gloria smiled. "Sarah, it's not healthy to keep everything all bottled up inside. It's a lot better to confide in someone you trust, like your brother."

"But I'm afraid Frank will be terribly upset. He's always been there to help me with my problems, but I don't know how he'll react to my letter. He'll probably hate me."

"He won't hate you. He'll undoubtedly hate Mike."

"No one in my family ever liked Mike. My parents hated him from the moment they met him. They didn't know how much he meant to me. Mike made me feel good about myself. He was kind and loving."

"Mike must have known you were starved for love and affection," Gloria said.

"Doesn't everyone want love and affection? Why am I so different?"

"You're not, but maybe you chose the wrong person to love."

"I don't think so," I answered, scowling. Then I placed my hands palm side down on my stomach, communicating with my unborn child. "I love my baby. I hope and pray that my brother can help me get Mike back."

"You're better off without him. Mike's no damn good. And I believe he's just been stringing you along."

"Look, Gloria, I know you're trying to help, but you don't understand how I feel. Mike's my baby's father. Without him I won't be able to keep my baby." As I spoke, I took a cigarette out of my purse and rummaged through my desk drawer for a match. When I found one, I lit the cigarette.

"You know you can't smoke in here," said Gloria. "You know it's against the rules."

"I don't give a damn about the rules." Stubbornly, I took several long drags from the cigarette and inhaled deeply. Thinking better of it then, I went into the bathroom and flushed the half-smoked cigarette down the toilet.

"Gloria," I mumbled, "I don't want to get you in trouble."

Four days later upon returning to my room after morning classes, I was surprised to see my brother's wife, Linda, waiting for me.

"What are you doing here?" I asked. "I wanted my brother to come for me."

"I'm sorry," said Linda, "but Frank couldn't get away, so he sent me instead." Then she held out her arms to me. I ran to her and cried like a baby. Gently, she rocked me to and fro as if I were a child in need of a loving mother. "Hush," she said, "everything's going to be all right. You're coming home with me to live with us. Your brother wants to help you."

Pulling away, I asked, "Does Frank hate me? Is he sorry I'm his sister?"

"Listen to me," Linda said, taking hold of my hand and looking into my face. "Your brother loves you very much. I'm sure he's glad you're his sister."

"What did he say when he read my letter?"

Pausing a moment, Linda said with a little sigh, "Well, he was stunned. He walked around the house and mumbled to himself. He paced the floor for hours. Then he read and reread your letter. Because he was upset, he couldn't sleep. It was past midnight when he finally came to bed. He tossed and turned all night."

"Oh, I knew he'd be upset. I never dreamed anything like this would happen to me. I never imagined I'd have to write Frank a letter and tell him I was pregnant. But I was desperate and didn't know what else to do."

"Sarah, you did the right thing. You had to tell someone, and your brother was a wise choice. Frank loves you. He wants you to be happy."

"The way I feel right now, well...I doubt if I'll ever be happy again. Oh, what's to become of me?"

"Let's take first things first and get you packed. You can think about the future later."

Fighting back the tears, I nodded.

"Are you all right?"

"I guess so, but I'm worried. Frank didn't tell Mother and Dad I'm pregnant, did he?"

"No, he didn't. Your parents are in New York City attending a convention."

"That's good."

"But, Sarah, eventually your parents will have to be told. For the moment you don't have to worry about them."

"What I'm concerned about is how I'm going to leave school. I can't walk out without an explanation."

"Your brother has already taken care of that. Frank spoke to the president of the college and explained that you're forced to leave school to have an operation resulting from a previous horse accident. Perhaps, dear, you should tell your friends the same thing."

"I don't want to see or talk to anyone. I just want to leave."

"I understand," said Linda as she helped me pack two small suitcases. "The rest of your things can be shipped," she added.

About twenty-five minutes later, Gloria walked in. She acted surprised and asked me what I was doing.

"I'm packing. I'm going home with my sister-in-law to live with her and my brother."

After I introduced Gloria to Linda, Gloria turned and faced me. There were tears streaming down her face. "I'm going to miss you," she murmured. She wiped the tears from her eyes and continued, "You've been a wonderful roommate. It won't be the same around here without you. Oh, I wish you could stay in school."

"So do I. No one regrets it more than I do, but I always knew I couldn't stay." Throwing my arms around Gloria, I whispered, "I don't know what I would have done without your friendship."

By this time I had finished packing and had closed my suitcases.

Sadly, I surveyed the room Gloria and I had shared. It was a typical-looking college girls' room with colorful bedspreads and matching drapes. The twin beds were piled high with stuffed animals of all colors and sizes. The walls were decorated with school banners. I had loved living here even though I had been unhappy most of the time. I hated to leave, but I realized I had no other choice. I was deep in thought when Linda asked me if I were ready to go.

"Yes," I said with a lump in my throat.

Without further hesitation, I quietly closed the door of my dormitory room, thus closing another chapter of my life. The three of us walked downstairs. Gloria and I hugged each other.

"Promise you'll keep in touch," she said.

"I promise."

"And, Sarah," she added, "I hope and pray that everything will work out all right for you."

"Thanks. I hope so, too."
I walked away and got into the car with Linda.
Linda turned the key in the ignition. We drove slowly down the long winding driveway, away from what I realized would have been an opportunity for a good education.

6

Love and Warm Milk

A s a new chapter of my life began, I did not look back. Instead, I looked straight ahead as each mile took me closer to my destination: my brother's house. Although I loved and trusted Frank, I was reluctant to face him. Shame and embarrassment pierced my heart because I knew that Frank knew I was pregnant. Yet I had always felt safe and secure with my brother. I looked up to him and believed he could fix anything that went wrong in my life. Now I was relying on him more than ever before.

Frank and Linda lived in a small town about 250 miles southwest of my parents' house. Frank was a vice president of a bank. I knew he and Linda had recently purchased their first house, which I was eager to see.

A day and a half later when Linda drove her car into the driveway and turned off the ignition, I got out and stretched. Stiff and tired from riding, I was glad the trip was over. I was excited about being there, but nervous, too. When I glanced toward the attractive, new ranch house, I saw Frank standing in the open doorway. He was smiling at me. Hurriedly, I ran to him.

Frank put his arms around me and hugged me. Then he turned his attention toward his wife. After greeting her with a kiss, he took the luggage from the trunk and escorted me into the living room.

"Come," he said, "sit over here." He motioned for me to sit next to him.

Frightened, I sat at the far end of the couch. I was self-counscious and afraid I would cry.

Frank seemed to understand that this was not an appropriate time to discuss my pregnancy. For a moment, he sat quietly and gazed at me. I felt like a scared little girl without a friend in the world.

"Sarah," he said, softly. "You must be tired. Perhaps it would be a good idea if you went to bed early."

"But I'm not tired," I protested. As I glanced out the corner of my eye at Frank, I thought he looked more like a college professor than a banker. He had a preppy look about him. Yet he had an unmistakable look of authority, too. Like Mother, his hair was blond with beautiful red highlights. His eyes were blue-green. He had a nice, friendly smile, yet I knew he also had a temper. When he was angry, he stuck his tongue in the side of his cheek and looked like a chipmunk. When he did that, there were times I was tempted to laugh. Instead, I scurried out of his way as quickly as possible. Thank goodness he was smiling now, I thought to myself.

The silence between us soon became awkward. Obviously, Frank didn't know what to say to me. He acted relieved when Linda came back into the room, took my hand, and led me down the hall.

When we came to the last door on the left, she stopped. "Sarah," she said, "this will be your room."

Wide-eyed, I looked into a beautiful bedroom where I saw French Provincial furniture, including a canopy bed. The large windows had pink chintz curtains that matched the canopy. The elegant rose color plush carpeting reminded me of cotton candy. Like a child who wanted to wade into a mountain stream, I sat down and took off my shoes and socks. When I stepped onto the carpeting, I was fascinated. – there were footprints in the pile.

"Oh, Linda! This room looks like it was meant for a fairy princess," I said.

"I'm glad you like it. Your brother and I want you to feel at home."

She then explained that my bathroom was down the hall, first door on the right, where I would find clean towels.

"If there's anything else you need, let me know."

"Thank you. And thanks a lot for coming down to school to get me."

"I was glad to do it," Linda said sweetly. "Even though you won't admit it," she added, "I know you're tired. So I'll leave you alone to get undressed and ready for bed."

The moment Linda left the room, I yawned and realized I was exhausted. Opening my suitcase, I pulled out a nightgown, bathrobe, and pair of slippers. I went down the hall to the bathroom and took a long, leisurely shower. Then I returned to my room and climbed into the canopy bed. I was about to fall asleep when I heard a knock on the door.

"Come in?"

When the door opened, I saw my brother. He was carrying a tray with a large glass of milk and a dish of cookies. "Linda thought you might be hungry," he said as he put the tray down on the night stand. "She told me to tell you to drink all the warm milk - it will help you sleep." Frank leaned down and kissed my forehead. "I'll see you in the morning," he said as he left the room.

"Warm milk - how disgusting!" I mumbled aloud. I thought about taking the glass of warm milk down the hall to the bathroom and flushing it down the toilet, but I didn't want to risk getting caught. Frowning, I closed my eyes, held my nose, and raised the glass to my lips. Cautiously, I took a tiny sip. Then I took another and another. To my surprise, the warm milk tasted good. Linda must have laced it with sugar and vanilla, I thought to myself. I finished drinking the milk and eating the cookies - all ten of them - and the next thing I knew the sun was coming up.

I opened my eyes and for a moment I was disoriented and wondered where I was. After a few seconds of confusion, I remembered I was in Frank and Linda's house. The aroma of freshly brewed coffee filtered through the air. I heard my brother whistling. Sunlight streamed into my room through the pink chintz curtains. The room looked warm and cozy, reminding me of my own home. Yawning, I threw my legs over the side of the canopy bed, but my feet didn't reach the floor. To get out of bed, I had to scoot over to the edge and gradually slither out. After I put on my robe and slippers, I made a quick trip down the hall and then into the kitchen where Linda was busily preparing breakfast. When she saw me, she smiled and asked how I had slept.

"I slept good. There must have been magic in that warm milk."

"I thought it would help you sleep. It always works for me," she said, motioning for me to sit at the kitchen table. "Breakfast will be ready in a minute," she added.

"But, Linda," I said. "I don't want anything to eat. I can't stand the sight or smell of food this early in the morning. I don't know why, but I get sick and throw up."

"What you're going through is perfectly normal," Linda explained. "Many women experience nausea and vomiting during their first two or three months of pregnancy. It's called morning sickness."

"No one bothered to tell me I'd be sick to my stomach every day for two or three months. No one bothered to tell me pregnancy was anything like this!"

Before I could say more, Frank, still whistling cheerfully, strolled into the kitchen. "Good morning, girls," he said as he pulled out a chair and sat opposite me.

Linda poured a cup of coffee for him and placed a large plate of food in front of him: scrambled eggs, hash-brown potatoes, sausage and hot buscuits smothered in thick milk gravy.

Sickened, I raised my hand to my mouth and ran down the hall to the bathroom. After throwing up, I splashed cold water onto my face, gargled with mouthwash and slowly returned to the kitchen.

Frank, who had finished eating breakfast, was reading the morning paper and smoking a cigarette.

"Are you all right?" he asked.

"I think so."

"That's good, because you and I have to talk about your future. We have to talk about your baby's future, too."

I had dreaded this moment, and even though I loved and respected my brother, I certainly didn't like the idea of discussing my pregnancy.

Nervously, I waited for Frank to speak.

"When is your baby due?" he asked.

"The first week in March, I think. Why?"

"Well, you're too far along to consider an abortion. You'll have to start thinking about placing your baby for adoption."

"I'm not going to place my baby for adoption. I love my baby, and I'm going to keep it."

"No, Sarah, you can't. If you did, both of you would be branded as social outcasts."

"But, Frank, I love Mike. If he and I were married, I could keep my baby."

I then explained that because I was adopted, I just couldn't bring myself to place my baby for adoption. "I've always been curious about my background. I don't want my child going through life wondering where he or she came from. And there's a strong bond of love between me and my baby," I told him. " For the first time in my life, I know what it feels like to be truly related to someone else."

"Marrying Mike to keep your baby would be foolish," Frank said. "You're too young to know what you want."

"I'm a grown woman who's pregnant. I want to get married and be out on my own like you and Linda."

"You're still just a child. I'm ten years older than you are, and believe me, when I was your age, marriage was the furthest thing from my mind. Mike took advantage of you! I wish I could get my hands on that bum – I'd wring his neck!"

It was Linda who interrupted Frank by saying, "Since Sarah is in love with Mike, perhaps you should pay him a visit and try to convince him to do the decent, honorable thing and marry your sister."

"She's too young to get married. She's still just a little girl."

"She's a pregnant little girl," Linda reminded him.

Frank looked at Linda. Then he looked at me.

"Well, Sarah," he said. "Since you're determined to marry Mike, and because you're pregnant, I'll do everything in my power to make it happen. I'll leave early tomorrow morning, and when I get back, I'll have Mike with me even if I have to drag him."

7

Waiting For My Beloved

The day Frank left to pay Mike a visit is a day I shall always remember. I believed my life was about to change for the better. Optimistic about the future, I felt good inside as I headed toward the bathroom to wash my hair.

"Not so fast," Linda said. "Before you wash your hair, I want you to wash the breakfast dishes."

"You can't boss me around."

"Now, let's get one thing straight; as long as you're living under my roof, I expect you to help me with the housework."

"This is Frank's house."

"Yes, and I'm Frank's wife."

"I know you're his wife, but in case you've forgotten, I'm his sister. I've been his sister a lot longer than you've been his wife."

"Sarah, you don't have to talk to me in that unpleasant tone of voice. I merely asked you to do the dishes."

"No, you didn't ask; you told me. If you had asked in a nice way, I would have responded differently."

"Well, I don't feel like arguing with you," Linda said. "From now on, it's your job to do the breakfast dishes and clean your room. Occasionally, I may ask you to dust the furniture. Do I make myself clear?"

"Yes," was my immediate reply.

Several hours later Linda and I drove into town to do the grocery shopping. When we finished, she suggested we stop at the corner drug store for an ice cream soda. Since I hadn't eaten breakfast, I was hungry. But every few minutes, I nervously glanced at my watch, since I worried about the meeting between Mike and my brother. Linda must have known I was anxious. She smiled sweetly and said, "Frank will do everything possible to convince Mike to come back with him."

"Oh, I'm not worried," I lied. "My brother always keeps his promises."

"Frank wants to keep his promise, but he's no miracle worker."

"My brother won't disappoint me. Did he ever tell you about the time Dad sold my horse, Lady?"

"He never mentioned it."

"Well, it was a long time ago when I was about ten years old. Mother had driven me out to the riding club so that I could exercise Lady in the ring. Without warning, Lady reared up and fell over backward on me."

"Is that the time you were hospitalized with a broken pelvis?"

"Yes, a broken pelvis, a broken arm and a broken leg."

"I've heard stories about that horse. Wasn't she a dangerous, high-spirited animal?"

"She was high-spirited, but very well trained. Before she was my horse, Lady belonged to Frank, who had trained her. The only reason she fell over backward was that one of the grooms had forgotten to put on her martingale. If he hadn't forgotten, Lady wouldn't have been able to rear."

"Why?" asked Linda.

"Because the martingale would have prevented her from throwing her head. Regardless, Dad blamed the horse for the accident and sold her. I was heartbroken. I wrote Frank, who was in the Naval Air Corps, and told him what had happened. He promised to buy Lady back for me. He kept that promise."

"I can see why you have so much faith in your brother, but buying a horse is quite different from arranging a marriage."

"I guess you don't know my brother as well as I do. Believe me, Frank always keeps his promise."

Twenty minutes later, Linda and I returned to the house. We unloaded the groceries and put them away. We sat down at the kitchen table, ate a sandwich, and relaxed with a cup of coffee. When lunch was finished, I complained, "Oh, this waiting is killing me. I can't sit still another minute."

"Why don't you take a walk?"

"I will. That's a good idea."

I put on a warm sweater and hurried out the door.

I noticed the leaves on the trees had started to turn color. There were shimmering golds, deep scarlets and brilliant yellows with a few dark green leaves mixed in for eye-pleasing contrast. When I looked up, I saw gray clouds. The clouds looked like mystical mountains casting their eerie shadows on the earth below.

I saw a herd of Guernsey cows busily chewing their cuds and standing head-to-head as if they were expecting a storm. I stopped to watch two cottontail rabbits scuttle across the road and head toward an open field to the safety of a deep furrow.

Then raindrops began to fall and moistened my face. I turned around and ran home. By the time I got there, I was soaked. Linda saw me and insisted that I take a hot shower so I wouldn't catch pneumonia.

After showering and drying my hair, I returned to my bedroom and climbed slowly into the canopy bed. Exhausted, I closed my eyes. The next thing I remember, Linda was shaking my shoulder.

"Sarah," she said, "it's time to get up. Your brother and Mike will be here soon."

Excitedly, I jumped down from the bed, grabbed a robe and ran down the hall to the bathroom. I stood in front of the mirror and wiped the sleep out of my eyes. After I washed my face, I carefully applied fresh make-up. I blotted my lips again and again so I wouldn't leave a smudge on Mike's face when I kissed him hello. I hurried to my room to get dressed. Then I went out the front door and sat on the steps to wait for Mike and my brother.

Each time a car approached, I prayed it was them. When it started to get dark, I pulled my knees up close to my chest and stretched my sweater down as far as it would go to keep warm. It didn't help much; I was still cold. I was about to give up the vigil and go inside when I saw the headlights of another car coming down the street toward me. Recognizing Frank's car, I jumped up and ran into the house.

"Linda, they're here! They're here!" I called out.

I rushed into the bathroom and checked my make-up. I put fresh perfume behind my ears as I had done so many times before while waiting for Mike. Then I walked down the hall toward the voices.

8

A Horrible Nightmare

The memory of the next moment will forever remain in my mind. I had expected to see Mike, but Frank was alone.

"Where is Mike?" I asked.

Hesitating before he answered, Frank looked directly into my face and whispered, "Sarah, I'm sorry, but he didn't come back with me."

"But, Frank!" I screamed, "You promised!"

"I know I did, but honestly, Sarah, you're better off without him. Mike's no damn good; he's a scoundrel."

"But I love him." I felt like I couldn't breathe. The room was closing in around me. My knees shook. I was dizzy and lightheaded. I had to hold onto a chair to keep from falling.

"Sarah, dear, come here and sit down," Linda suggested.

"No, I don't want to sit down."

"Sit down before you fall down," Frank ordered. Without giving me a chance to argue, he pulled me down onto the couch next to him.

"Frank, tell me what happened," I begged. It was then I noticed Frank's right hand was black and blue with badly bruised knuckles.

"Oh, Frank," I said. "You didn't hit Mike, did you? Oh, Lord, you got into a fight with him. That's why he didn't come back. Frank, how could you...?"

"Yes, Sarah, I hit him, but that's not the reason he didn't come back with me."

"What other reason could there be?"

"I'm sorry to tell you, Sarah, but Mike has married another woman."

"I don't believe you. You're teasing..."

"No, Sarah, I wouldn't tease about something as serious as this."

"Well, I just can't believe what I'm hearing."

"I'm sorry," Linda said, sympathetically.

After echoing his wife's sentiment, Frank continued, "I knew you'd be devastated when you found out, and that's why I slugged him. The last time I saw Mike, he was sprawled out on the floor."

"I'm glad you hit him! I wish I could hit him! How could I have been so stupid? And to think I thought Mike was an honorable man just like you and Dad."

"Sarah, dear," Linda said, "there are very few men in this world who are as honest and decent as your father and brother. Unfortunately, most young men are out for a good time. I thought you knew that."

"I did, but I never dreamed Mike was one of them."

"It's despicable that he married another woman," Linda commented, "and I'm sick about it, but now we have to concentrate on your future."

"What future? Without Mike, I have no future, and part of me will always love him."

"I told you - you're better off without him," Frank reiterated. "He wouldn't have been a good husband for you or a good father for your baby."

"That's beside the point!" I screamed, losing my temper. "He is my baby's father and nothing can ever change that!"

"Forget about him. You're young. You have your entire life ahead of you. Take my advice and start thinking about placing your baby for adoption."

"No, Frank, I'm keeping my baby."

"You can't!"

"But you don't understand how I feel. My baby belongs to me. I can't give it away."

"You must think about what's best for your baby," Linda said, putting her arm around my shoulder in an attempt to comfort me. Stubbornly, I pulled away.

"What's wrong with me?" I yelled. "Why didn't Mike marry me?"

"Nothing's wrong with you," Frank said. "Mike told me that he and the girl he married had gone together all through high school and college. Evidently they had been engaged, but a few weeks before he met you, they had had an argument and she broke their engagement. After several months passed and she realized she was pregnant, she got in touch with him. Three days later, they were married."

"She's expecting his baby? I feel like a damn fool!"

"Perhaps you acted foolishly, but you're no fool," said Frank. "You're an inexperienced young woman who made a mistake by trusting an older man. Mike was playing games with you. More importantly, he was afraid of your parents. Since you're underage, he was worried Mother and Dad would find out about your pregnancy and cause him trouble."

"Mike spoke about my age often, but why did he come down to school to see me if he were planning to marry someone else?"

"He told me he had tried to tell you about it, but when you threatened to write to me, he panicked."

"Oh, Frank, this is like a horrible nightmare. What am I going to do?"

"As I told you, Sarah, you must place your baby for adoption."

"How many times do I have to tell you I won't do that. You don't understand how I feel because you're not adopted. Sometimes I look into the mirror and stare at myself. I wonder if there's anyone in the world who looks like me. I think about my real mother and wonder why she gave me away."

"She undoubtedly loved you enough to give you a normal life with a respectable family. Obviously, she put her personal feelings aside so that you would have a good life. She did what she had to do."

"But, Frank, you still don't understand. I don't know who I am. I don't even know what nationality I am. I don't know anything about my background. There have been times when I've thought I'd go crazy if I didn't find answers to questions most people take for granted. Simple things like: where was I born? What time was I born? How much did I weigh? Did my real mother see me? Did she hold me in her arms? Did she love me? I've wondered about so many things. It's like chasing rainbows, hoping to find a pot of gold that will hold all the answers."

"Well, Sarah, I must admit that I don't understand exactly how you feel. Regardless, you're wrong to even consider keeping your baby. Society is cruel. Society won't allow a young, unmarried woman to raise a baby. I've told you and I'll tell you again: you must think about what's best for your child."

"Damn! You're like everyone else in the world who isn't adopted! I could talk until I'm blue in the face and you wouldn't understand how I feel. You don't have the foggiest idea where I'm coming from. Only people who are adopted would understand. But I hope you understand this – I'm going to fight with every ounce of strength in my body to keep my baby!"

9

Doesn't Anyone Listen?

The time came that I realized I had to forget about Mike and my shattered dreams. I knew I couldn't allow depression or self-pity to consume all my days and nights. For my baby's sake, I had to force myself to have a brighter outlook on life. It wasn't long until I felt my baby move for the very first time. Thrilled, I ran to tell Linda about it.

"Oh, it's a strange new feeling like the fluttering of a tiny butterfly. It's a wonderful sensation - a miracle!"

"Sarah," Linda said, "when I look at you, I see a little girl. It's impossible for me to think of you as a mother."

Shrugging, I placed my hands on my stomach and whispered, "Your mother loves you, baby."

Less than a week later, Frank informed me he thought our parents should be told that I was living with him and Linda. "And we must tell them you're pregnant," he added.

"I can't be the one to tell them."

"Linda and I talked it over and decided it would be best if I went to see them."

"Please, Frank, can't we put off telling them?"

"No, Mother and Dad have a right to know."

"Well, I don't want to be anywhere around when you talk to them."

"Don't worry, that's why you're staying here with Linda. And after this trip, Sarah, I can't take any more time away from my work."

When Frank left to see my parents, I started worrying. I bit my fingernails, paced the floor, and twisted my hair. "I don't envy Frank this trip," I told Linda. "I know there's no easy way for him to tell Mother and Dad I'm expecting a baby."

"You're right," Linda agreed. "Frank loves you, but he loves his parents, too. He told me he feels caught in the middle."

"I know it's hard on my brother, but doesn't anyone care about what I'm going through? I'm the one who's suffering. I'm the one who's having a baby. But since I'm still a minor, no one bothers to ask me what I want. No one understands how much I love my baby. Frank wants me to place it for adoption because he knows Mother and Dad don't love me enough to let me keep it - especially Mother."

"Your mother loves you, Sarah. Sometimes I believe she loves you too much. However, when she finds out what a mess you've made of your life, she'll undoubtedly be terribly upset. I'm sure she'll agree with Frank about placing your baby for adoption."

"Doesn't anyone ever listen to me? I'm keeping my baby!"

"I think it would be foolish to try. Not only foolish, but selfish, too."

"Well, I don't give a hoot what you think. And I'm not going to stay here another minute listening to you."

I remember as if it were yesterday. I stayed in my room the rest of the day, wondering and worrying what my parents would say when they learned their daughter - their adopted daughter - was pregnant. I was sure my mother would hate me; my father, I believed, would be shocked. Worrying myself into mental exhaustion, it wasn't long until I fell asleep.

I slept so soundly that I didn't hear Frank come home later that evening. The next morning when I awoke, I asked him about his visit with Mother and Dad.

"Sarah, I've never seen them so upset. Mother cried - Dad cried, too."

"I never meant to hurt them. I never meant to hurt anyone," I said, tears forming in the corners of my eyes.

"Don't you dare start crying," Frank warned. "I can't tolerate your tears right now. I'm worn out and my nerves are shot."

"But what about me? What about my feelings?"

Suddenly, without warning, Frank took hold of my shoulders and shook me. Although he didn't shake me hard, he hurt my pride, and in spite of his warning, I started to cry.

Then he looked at me and said, kindly, "I know you didn't set out to hurt anyone, but your pregnancy has affected many other people. Mother and Dad couldn't be more shocked or upset; they wanted so much for you..."

I interrupted, "I knew they'd be furious when they found out I quit school because I was pregnant. Now they probably wish they'd never adopted me."

"They're disappointed in you, Sarah. Mother believes you don't appreciate a good family."

"She'd feel differently if I were her flesh-and-blood daughter. She feels the way she does because I'm adopted."

"Sarah, sit down and shut up!"

Knowing Frank was angry, I sat down.

He looked directly into my eyes and said, "I'm sick and tired of hearing you complain about being adopted. You don't realize how fortunate you are to have wonderful parents like ours who love us both."

"They love you, but they don't love me."

"I thought I told you to be quiet."

Silence followed.

"You don't appreciate Mother and Dad," Frank went on. "You don't understand they've given you many opportunities denied most children. You've been sent to the very best private girls' schools available. You've always lived comfortably in a large, luxurious house with a maid to pick up after you, and..."

"That's not true! Mother doesn't allow Hettie to clean my room."

Ignoring my interruption, Frank continued to speak. "You have a beautiful show horse to ride. You belong to the best country clubs in town. Mother sees to it that you have expensive clothes to wear and Dad bought you a new car to drive. When I was your age, I had to work hard to pay for my first car. Everything has been handed to you. You've had social, moral, and financial advantages most people only dream about. And what do you do about it? You throw it all away for some jerk you think you're in love with. To make matters worse, you have the audacity to complain about being adopted."

"I know Mother and Dad buy me nice things and send me to good schools, but they never tell me they love me."

"You shouldn't have to be told. You're smart enough to know Mother and Dad love you. There are times, Sarah, when I feel like taking you over my knee and spanking you."

"But, Frank...."

"Don't 'but, Frank' me. I've tried to understand you, but most of the time I don't. Perhaps you need answers to your questions concerning your biological history. Maybe some day when you're older you'll find those answers. But in the meantime, young lady, count your blessings! I don't want to hear you complain *ever again* about being adopted!"

What happened next will forever remain a grim memory. Frank informed me Mother and Dad had agreed to let me stay with him and Linda until three weeks before my baby was due.

"Then Dad will come for you and he'll take you to a maternity home for unwed mothers," Frank explained.

"I won't go."

"Yes, you will."

"No! I'll run away first!"

"You have nowhere to run. Besides, the maternity home for unwed mothers, near where Mother and Dad live, is a very nice place. Although they are brokenhearted, Mother and Dad want you to have the best medical care possible. You're to stay at the home and deliver your baby. Then you must place it for adoption."

"I can't give my baby away."

"You must. Mother and Dad love you, and they're concerned about your baby's future and yours, too."

"No one in my family loves me. But my real mother does, and some day - I swear - I'm going to find her."

10

Two Outcasts at Christmas

T he ensuing weeks passed quickly as I settled into the day-in-day-out life with my brother and his wife. The memories of the time spent with them are enjoyable, with much laughter and sunshine. Frank remained kind and considerate. Linda and I became good friends.

Thanksgiving came and went. Christmas was only a week away. Everyone except me was caught up in the holiday spirit and looking forward to the festivities. I was upset because Frank and Linda planned to spend Christmas Day with my parents at Aunt Adaline's house.

Aunt Adaline was my mother's oldest sister. She lived about sixty five miles south of my parents' house. Because I was wearing maternity clothes, I couldn't go with them. Frank made it clear that Mother and Dad didn't want to see me, nor did they want anyone in the family to see me or know my whereabouts. All my aunts, uncles and cousins were invited, but I wasn't included. I felt as if I were carrying a communicable disease. I hated my parents for what I believed was an antiquated attitude toward my pregnancy.

"I feel as though I don't belong to this family," I told Frank.

He looked at me with a glare of disapproval on his usually tranquil face, preventing me from elaborating. I was afraid I would hear critical words from him.

Linda tried to coax me into helping her trim the Christmas tree.

"I can't force myself to look at the tree," I said. "I wish I could close my eyes and make Christmas disappear."

"I'm sorry you feel that way," Linda replied.

"Well, I do. I don't know why everyone is making such a big fuss about Christmas - it's just another day."

Although I refused to help, Linda spent two days decorating the six foot tall tree. Her task completed, she put the ladder away, stood back and admired her masterpiece. I thought the tree was elegantly trimmed, but I wasn't interested in the Christmas tree or the beautifully wrapped gifts under it.

That evening, Linda fixed a Christmas dinner especially for me - baked ham with raisin sauce, candied sweet potatoes, green beans, a fruit salad and my favorite dessert, pumpkin pie. But I wasn't hungry. Half way through the meal, I excused myself and disappeared into my room.

The next morning as I hid behind the drapes in the living room and watched Frank and Linda drive away, the dam inside my heart gave way to a flood of tears. Sad and lonely, I spent the entire day in bed. Sleep finally came. I didn't awaken until the following morning - Christmas Day.

Slowly, I got out of bed and stretched. The house was cold and damp. I heard strange noises I had never heard before. Shivering, I walked into the kitchen and fixed a pot of coffee. Then I noticed Frank's car keys hanging on the wall by the back door. (Frank and Linda had driven Linda's car.) I stared at the keys. Taking them down from the wall, I tossed them into the air. As I caught them, I decided to take my brother's car and drive home. I knew I would have the house all to myself, since everyone else had gone to Aunt Adaline's. I felt as if something bigger than I were pulling me home. I dressed, checked the ashtrays to make certain all the cigarettes were out, and then got into my brother's car and started driving.

The highway was deserted, since everyone else had reached his destination, I thought to myself. Turning on the radio, I listened as a choir sang "Silent Night". I turned it off. I wasn't in the mood for Christmas music. Two monotonous hours later, I pulled in front of my house.

As I got out of the car and walked to the front door, although I didn't want to think about him, I reminisced about Mike. I thought about the many times he had kissed me good night. I remembered when he held me in his arms. I remembered the times we made love. The passion I thought would never die seemed a lifetime ago. Thinking about him hurt. Deliberately pushing the painful memory of Mike out of my mind, I found my key and unlocked the door. When I walked into the entry-hall, I heard someone call out, "Who's there?"

"Grandmother, is that you?" I asked as I ran upstairs. An instant later, I found my grandmother standing by her bedroom door. She was trembling all over.

"Oh, I never meant to frighten you. Are you all right?"

"Yes, dear," she answered.

"Why didn't you go with the rest of the family?"

"It isn't easy for me to travel anymore, child. And I didn't want to ruin everyone else's Christmas."

"They shouldn't have left you here alone..."

"I'm perfectly all right," she assured me.

Suddenly I remembered I was wearing maternity clothes. Taking a few steps backward, I drew my coat securely around myself in a desperate attempt to conceal my pregnancy from my grandmother.

"Sarah, dear," she said. "You needn't hide from me. I heard your parents talking about what happened to you. I know you're expecting a baby."

Surprised that she knew, I swallowed hard. I didn't know what to say.

Smiling sweetly, she extended her hand - a small, fragile-looking hand that was badly crippled with arthritis. Then she invited me into her bedroom. "Come, dear. We'll have a nice, long talk just like we used to do when you were a little girl."

As I followed her into her bedroom, I said, "Oh, Grandmother, I was afraid if you ever found out I was pregnant, you wouldn't love me anymore."

"Nonsense, child. Nothing could change my love for you. You're my granddaughter. I'll always love you."

"I never wanted this to happen," I blurted out. "It's like a horrible car accident. You don't think it will happen to you. But, Grandmother, I was in love with Mike. I trusted him..."

"I know, dear, and I'm truly sorry."

"Thanks, Grandmother. You've always been understanding, but I'm worried about Mother and Dad. I doubt if they'll ever forgive me."

"In time they will. Right now, they're disturbed and terribly disheartened. Your mother is convinced you've ruined your life. And, Sarah, she had such wonderful dreams for you. You've destroyed all the visions of grandeur she had for you, and she blames herself."

"Why?"

"Because she thinks she failed you somewhere along the way. Night after night I've heard her crying. She asks your father often where she went wrong. Your mother loves you, Sarah."

"But she never tells me she loves me."

"The words 'I love you' are difficult for some people to say aloud. There are folk who are unable to verbalize their feelings. I'm afraid your mother is one of them. However, she shows her love in other ways. She loves you more than most mothers would."

"That's news to me."

"Don't be too hard on your mother, Sarah. She and your father love you very much."

"No, they don't."

"It makes me sad," said Grandmother, "that you don't recognize the love your parents have for you. I'll always remember how happy they were when they adopted you. They waited years, and when you were born, you were very ill with yellow jaundice. Babies who didn't have a clean bill of health couldn't be placed for adoption. Your parents waited *four* months before they were allowed to bring you home. Meanwhile, they paid your medical bills and prayed you'd recover."

"They did...?"

"Yes, and I still remember the day they brought you home from the hospital. When your mother held you in her arms, her eyes were full of mother love for her baby. She couldn't have loved you more if you had been born to her. The bonding was there between mother and child. No one knows better than I how much your mother truly loves you."

"Well, if she does, I'd like to hear her say the words. Until then, I'll be doubtful. Besides, if Mother loved me, she'd let me keep my baby."

"Love has nothing to do with your mother's decision. She wants you to place your baby for adoption because she's a wise woman. She realizes your child deserves a mother and a father. Your mother realizes, too, that bringing up a child under normal, everyday circumstances is a big responsibility..."

"I don't give a .... I don't care what my mother thinks. I'm keeping my baby."

"You can't always have what you want, Sarah. Sometimes, dear, you must think about what is best for others."

"But, Grandmother, it's almost 1949 - times are changing. I believe the day will come when girls who have babies out of wedlock will keep them. And no one will say a word about it."

"Oh, no, Sarah, you're wrong," Grandmother said, reaching for my hand and gently squeezing it. She told me I should learn to trust in the Lord. "I'm glad," she added, "that I accepted a simple faith in God and the teachings of the Bible before the age of doubt and questioning. If a person has faith, it will see her through the difficult times."

Silently, I reflected on what my grandmother had said.

The day passed quickly. Grandmother and I enjoyed each other's company. I forgot, for awhile, about my problems. I was happy.

That evening, I fixed Grandmother and myself a good dinner. I didn't think my mother would ever miss the ham I took from the refrigerator. I slept comfortably in my own room in my own bed. The next morning when I awoke, the sun had risen - Christmas was over.

After carefully making the bed so that no one would suspect I had slept there, I ran downstairs and made coffee. Grandmother and I visited for awhile, and then I knew it was time to leave. Unwanted tears blurred my vision.

"Please, don't cry," Grandmother said. "If only you knew how happy you've made me, you'd be happy, too. Having you with me has been the best Christmas gift anyone has ever given me."

"Thank you, Grandmother," I said, kissing her goodbye.

She gave me a hug and whispered softly, "Sarah, dear, I'll see you again soon."

11

If Mother Loved Me

On the return trip, traffic was heavy. I didn't relax until I drove into the driveway and parked my brother's car in the garage where it belonged. Because Frank and Linda were expected home later that same day, I was relieved I had arrived first.

Hurriedly, I walked into the living room and opened the gifts they had left for me. There was a heart-shaped gold locket, a portable record player, and several records, one of which was "Rhapsody in Blue" by George Gershwin. I loved anything written by Gershwin. His haunting music had a unique sound of honesty and simplicity. Although I was grateful the holidays were over, I was pleased with my gifts and knew I would always remember the Christmas season I spent with my brother and his wife.

January and February seemed to fly by. Since I had carried my baby almost nine months, I felt as if I had gone from girlhood to womanhood practically overnight, never to recapture my youth.

The day my father came for me I wanted to run away. I loved Dad and had missed him terribly, but I didn't want to face him. I was embarrassed because I was large, extremely clumsy and walked like a fat, bow-legged duck.

After he visited with Frank and Linda, Dad turned his attention to me. "Sarah," he said, "are you packed and ready to leave?"

"Yes, I guess so," I answered. I noticed he didn't look directly at me. Instead he looked past, around and over me. I could see an undeniable sadness in his gentle gray-blue eyes. He acted as if he, too, were embarrassed. He was nervous and insisted we get started as soon as possible.

When the time came to say goodbye to the life I had become accustomed to with Frank and Linda, I wept. I hugged Frank so hard that he finally had to pry my arms away. I loved him as a brother, but since we weren't truly related to one another, I had always secretly loved him as a man, too. Yet I had become fond of Linda. When I told her goodbye, I gave her a hug. Then I got into the car with my father and we started on our journey.

After we had driven for a short time, I turned to Dad and asked him about my mother. "I've missed Mother," I said. "How is she?"

"Your mother isn't well."

"I'm sorry, Dad."

"Saying you're sorry doesn't help much. What's more," he said, "I don't understand why you disgraced our good name, after all we've done for you."

"Well, Dad, I don't understand why Mother wants me to give my baby away. I've heard people say they have a broken heart, but I never knew what those words meant until now. My heart is breaking. I hurt. If Mother loved me, she would help me keep my baby."

"Your mother is thinking, as usual, about what is best for you. She was the one who wanted you to have a good education. It was your mother who insisted you be sent to the best girls' schools."

"I didn't want to go to private school. I wanted to go to public school like my cousins. No one ever asked me what I wanted."

"Sarah, you have never appreciated what your mother has done for you. It was your mother who bought you your Welsh pony, Duchess."

I stared at Dad in surprise. I had always believed he was the one who had purchased Duchess. As I thought about the pony I had loved so much, tears came to my eyes. Then there was silence between us. The only sounds that could be heard above the purr of the car motor were the weird sounds coming from my upset stomach. I had a headache that got worse as we drove closer and closer to my Gethsemane. About an hour and half later, we arrived at the maternity home for unwed mothers.

After Dad parked the car, he got out and took my suitcases and record player from the trunk.

I couldn't move, as if frozen to the front seat. I looked out the car window at the large brick building perched high on a hill. It was a three-story building that resembled a mansion. I noticed steep cement steps leading up to the front door, and a pine tree growing out of the side of the hill. The tree had puny, twisted branches reaching toward the sky. The sight of the deformed-looking tree made me shudder. My heart beat like a kettle drum. A chill ran down my spine.

Moments later, Dad opened the car door and helped me out. I stood motionless. Then he instructed me to follow him up the steps that led to what would be my new home. Reluctantly, I obeyed him. When we reached the top, I was out of breath. I looked down the hill and wished I could return to the safety of my father's car, but he took my arm and escorted me through the front door.

We found ourselves in a dark hallway. It took a minute or two to adjust our eyes to the shadows surrounding us. I heard the sound of footsteps coming toward us. The click, click, click of high heels on polished hardwood floors became louder and louder. A woman appeared, shook hands with my father and introduced herself. "Good evening. I'm Mrs. Anderson, the administrator. I've been expecting you. Sarah's room is ready for her." As she spoke, she took us into a large, lavishly furnished parlor where the sound of our footsteps was muffled by thick, gray carpeting. My legs ached from the long climb, and I was glad to have the opportunity to sit down.

Dad put my suitcases and record player on the floor beside my chair. He handed me three twenty dollar bills. Reaching into his pocket, he pulled out a handful of loose change and gave them to me, also.

"Thank you, Dad," I said as I put the money into my purse.

"I'm going to leave you now," Dad whispered. He kissed my cheek. Then, without another word, he turned and walked away.

Frightened and apprehensive, I was left alone with Mrs. Anderson, a stout middle-aged woman with an annoying high-pitched voice. She wore a brown business suit that looked two or three sizes too small. Her offensive perfume made me want to sneeze, but try as I might, a sneeze wouldn't come. Her lipstick looked as though she had forgotten to blot it, and she wore too much rouge on her chubby little cheeks. She looked top-heavy with bosoms that rose and fell as she breathed. I decided I didn't like this woman. I didn't like the way she talked, the way she dressed or the way she wore her bleached blond hair pulled back away from her face, exposing her over-sized pierced ears.

"My dear," said Mrs. Anderson in her nerve-wracking voice that sounded like fingernails on a chalk board, "I want to tell you something about the maternity home. It's very important that you remember everyone here, including most of the staff members, use only their first names. Confidentiality is a must. Do you understand?"

"Yes."

"Splendid," Mrs. Anderson said. She then informed me all the girls who came here did so voluntarily so that they could place their babies for adoption. "All our girls," she went on to explain, "have been personally recommended by their physicians or ministers."

"How nice."

Nodding, she told me the girls were from fine, respectable, prominent families. "We have girls who are bankers' daughters, lawyers' daughters, ministers' daughters, physicians' daughters and insurance executives' daughters." Pausing to catch her breath, she asked if I had any questions.

"No, Ma'am," I answered. I didn't have any questions, nor did I want to converse with this woman. But she, unaware of my reluctance to communicate, kept talking.

"Our girls have chosen to place their babies for adoption because they know it's best for the baby. It's a well-known fact that having a baby out of wedlock is unacceptable in today's society. Our girls come here, deliver their babies, place them for adoption, and when they go home, they try to forget about the past and go on with their lives."

It sounded as though Mrs. Anderson thought she knew what was best for me and my baby. She talked as if I had a broken leg that would heal, allowing me to throw away the cast and go on with my life as if nothing had happened. I resented her nonchalant attitude. I hadn't given up hope that Mother would change her mind and allow me to keep my baby. What woman with any heart at all could resist a newborn, I asked myself. While I was preoccupied thinking about my mother, Mrs. Anderson was busy talking. I had a headache and wanted to put my hands over my ears to escape her incessant chattering. She must have sensed that I wasn't paying attention because she began speaking even louder.

"All our girls eat their meals in the dining room, cafeteria style," she told me. Suddenly, her voice was drowned out by the sound of a loud bell.

"Don't be frightened," she said. "That's our dinner bell. I'm sorry if it startled you."

My attention was distracted. I glanced toward the hall and saw several pregnant girls walking by. When they saw me sitting there with Mrs. Anderson, a few of them waved and smiled. Some were small, obviously not far along into their pregnancies, while others looked as if they were going to deliver their babies momentarily. I had never before seen so many pregnant girls. As I watched them file by, I became dizzy and lightheaded. My palms were sweaty. My stomach felt queasy.

I closed my eyes; that's all I remember.

12

You Can Have
Another Baby

When I regained consciousness, my vision was blurred, and I was disoriented. Was it my imagination or was there an angel hovering over me?

"Did I die and go to heaven?" I asked softly.

"No, dear, you're very much alive."

"Where am I?"

"You're in your room at the maternity home."

"How did I get here?"

"When you fainted, Mrs. Anderson had one of the orderlies carry you upstairs."

"Oh," I said. I looked around at the unfamiliar surroundings. Opening my eyes wider, I saw that the "angel" was a woman dressed in a nurse's uniform. She was tall and slender with almond-shaped hazel eyes. Her beautiful oval face had delicate features. Her flawless complexion glowed. When she smiled, she tilted her head to one side and displayed a deep dimple in her left cheek. She had a small, turned-up nose and the prettiest red hair I had ever seen. Her hair was piled high on her head with a few loose strands stubbornly escaping into ringlets at the nape of her graceful neck. When she spoke, her voice was barely above a whisper, but I could hear her every word. When I looked at her again, I thought she did, indeed, resemble an angel.

"You're going to be all right," she assured me. Then she sat down on the edge of my bed and hugged me. The warmth of her arms comforted me. I felt protected like a child being held by her mother.

"My name is Gladys," she said. "I'm the resident nurse here." Her kind soothing voice quieted my fears. Immediately I felt better and believed I had found a friend.

Suddenly, the door opened. I looked up to see a pregnant girl carrying a dinner tray which she placed on my night stand. Smiling, she introduced herself.

"Hi, my name's Kathy. I'm your roommate. Mrs. Anderson told me you fainted. I hope you're feeling better now."

"I'm feeling much better, thank you," I said. When I introduced myself to her, I almost forgot the first-name-only rule, but stopped before I mentioned my last name.

Gladys looked affectionately at the two of us. "Sarah," she said, "I'll leave you in Kathy's good hands. But if you need me for anything, come to the front desk."

After Gladys left the room, I felt as though I were all alone in a foreign land. Frowning, I thought about my parents as I ate dinner. I hated them for sending me here.

Kathy, obviously thrilled to have a captive audience, talked on and on like a magpie. She told me she had been confined to the home for five and a half months. "My baby's due in four weeks," she said with a long, drawn-out sigh.

"Mine's due in three weeks," I told her.

"Well, I don't know how you feel," she went on, "but I can hardly wait until this dreadful ordeal is behind me. Then I can go on with my life. I can't wait to go home! But before I go, my mother's taking me on a Caribbean cruise so that I'll look healthy and tan when I face my family and friends. Everyone thinks I've been vacationing in Europe."

"What about your baby? Have you considered keeping it?"

"I'm too young to worry about a baby. My mother keeps telling me I'm still just a child myself. She wants me to finish college. Then someday when I'm older, she wants me to marry into a prominent, wealthy family. *Then* I can start thinking about having a baby. I wouldn't want to be tied down now."

Kathy was an attractive girl, probably in her early twenties, with an outgoing personality. It was obvious she came from a good home and had been given a good education. However, she seemed self-centered and a bit snobbish. But I liked her. It was good to have someone my age to talk to. I decided to tell her I wanted to keep my baby.

Raising her eyebrows, Kathy stared at me in disbelief.

"If you keep your baby, you'll always be sorry."

"No, I won't be sorry..."

"Well, I can't think of anything worse than taking care of a screaming infant. Where would you live? How would you manage?"

"I want my parents to adopt my baby. That way," I explained, "I can keep it. But I guess you don't understand how I feel."

"No, I don't," Kathy responded. "I don't understand why anyone in her right mind would want to change dirty diapers."

"I have my reasons."

"I can't think of even one good reason."

"I don't want to place my baby for adoption because I'm adopted."

"You are...you're adopted?"

"Yes, and I know how it feels. I've always felt different, as if there's a part of my life that's missing. I don't want my baby to feel..."

"Why didn't you marry your baby's father?" Kathy interrupted.

"Because he married someone else."

"I'm sorry," said Kathy.

"Thanks, but for months I've heard people say they're sorry. Sorry doesn't help much."

"Sarah, you're young. One of these days, you'll meet a nice guy, fall in love, and get married. Then you can have another baby."

"But I want this one."

"You're nuts!" Kathy said as she walked to her dresser and pulled out the bottom drawer. Reaching inside, she took out a skimpy black bathing suit. "Do you see this?" she asked, impishly.

"Yes...?"

"After my baby's born, I'm going to fit into this bathing suit or die trying. I'm sick of looking like a fat cow." Kathy stood in front of her mirror, held the suit at arm's length and admired it.

I excused myself and took a shower. The warm water pulsating over my body felt good against the stretch marks on my upper thighs and abdomen. When I finished bathing, I put on a nightgown and was getting into bed when Gladys reappeared.

"I'm going off duty now," she said. "I hope you girls get a good night's sleep."

I lay awake feeling lost and depressed. Finally, I turned my face toward the wall. Silent tears moistened my pillow.

13

Second Choice

When I awoke the next morning, I realized the living conditions were, indeed, as my brother had told me - very nice. The room I shared with Kathy was similar to the one I had in college. It was furnished with twin beds, mirrored dressers, two chests of drawers, two lounge chairs, and a desk. Kathy and I shared the adjoining bathroom and a large walk-in closet. The room was tastefully decorated in pastel colors.

I learned from Mrs. Anderson that the home was founded in the early 1900s by a woman who wanted to help an unwed mother, a frightened young girl who had nowhere to go. It was now owned and operated by a prominent physician. There were five staff doctors, four registered nurses, a social worker, a dietitian, and Mrs. Anderson, the administrator. Because I was curious about the home and the girls who came there, I questioned my roommate.

Kathy seemed delighted to have the opportunity to tell me everything she knew. "There's a lot of snob appeal about this particular home," she said. "My mother told me the home is like the Ritz or the Waldorf for unwed mothers. She also said it cost more to stay here than to attend a girls' finishing school."

It had never occurred to me that my parents were spending a large sum of money for my confinement. This worried me. Now they would have another reason to be angry.

Shrugging off my fears, however, I asked Kathy about the girls. Prior to coming here, I assumed I would be surrounded by young women who had terrible reputations, perhaps even prostitutes. I was greatly relieved to learn from Mrs. Anderson that all the girls were from homes comparable to mine - girls who, like me, had made mistakes by trusting the wrong man. Now I was eager to learn more about the girls.

"Well," said Kathy, taking a long breath, "there's forty-five of us living here now. We're all about the same age – in our late teens or early twenties. But there's one girl who's only twelve years old."

"Isn't she a little young?"

"Yes, and to make matters worse, she's a deaf girl who was badly beaten and raped. She stays in her room with a private nurse who takes care of her. It's sad – she doesn't fully understand what happened to her."

"The poor kid," was all I could manage to say.

Nodding in agreement, Kathy told me about another girl in her late thirties. "She wears a wedding ring. Every day at exactly two o'clock in the afternoon, a tall, handsome man comes to see her. When he leaves, she runs to her room and cries. We're curious about him, and some of us think he's her husband, but we don't ask any questions."

"Maybe she's a wealthy married woman who had an affair. The man who visits her could be her secret lover. Perhaps she told her husband she was vacationing in some exotic faraway land so that she could sneak away, come here, give birth to her baby, and maybe..."

"And maybe you have an overactive imagination," Kathy teased.

"So I've been told," I answered.

Then Kathy told me about another girl named Bonnie who was engaged to be married. "Bonnie told all of us that as soon as her baby is born, she's placing it for adoption. Afterward, she plans to marry immediately. We think her baby belongs to someone other than her fiancé, but we don't ask her any questions either."

As Kathy kept talking, I learned all the girls except me were from out of town. They had come from small communities and large metropolitan areas scattered all over the United States. Some of them had traveled long distances from their homes to hide from family and friends, thus keeping their pregnancies a secret. Most of them, according to Kathy, were college students who planned to return to school after their babies were born.

I also learned the maternity home was divided into two sections. The front part, where Kathy and I lived, was for the girls who had parents or guardians who could afford to pay handsomely for their confinement. The back part was for the girls who had to work to pay their way.

"The rooms in the back section are small and dreary-looking," Kathy said. "The girls who live there work in the laundry room, the kitchen, the cafeteria, or the nursery. A few of them work as nurse's aids."

As I listened to Kathy, we walked downstairs and headed toward the cafeteria for breakfast. Then Kathy told me the food was awful. Elaborating, she said the only time the food was edible was when the doctor who owned the home was on the premises.

When we reached the cafeteria and started down the line, I was surprised to see quite a variety of food to choose from: English muffins, cinnamon rolls, toast and jelly. Farther down the line there were scrambled eggs, sausage and bacon. There were fruit juices, coffee, tea and milk. I chose scrambled eggs, coffee and a small glass of juice. Then I followed Kathy to an empty table.

Because the cafeteria was deserted, I asked Kathy where the other girls were.

"Most of them sleep late. Breakfast is the only meal we're allowed to skip."

"What do we do the rest of the day to occupy our time?" I asked.

"Not much of anything."

"How boring!"

"Well," said Kathy, "I suppose you could say we're ladies-in-waiting who are lazily lying around, waiting for our babies to be born. However," she went on to say, "there's a day room on the second floor where we can play cards, work puzzles, visit, or listen to the radio. Most of us prefer to stay in our rooms and read a good book. We've been warned by Mrs. Anderson not to exchange last names, addresses or telephone numbers. And we've been told repeatedly not to become friends."

"I can't believe I'm stuck in a place like this," I muttered as my spirits plummeted to depths never before reached. Looking up , I saw Gladys enter the room.

"Good morning," she said, smiling. She pulled out a chair and sat down next to me. Still smiling sweetly, she asked me how I felt.

"Oh, I feel bad. I know that everyone here expects me to place my baby for adoption. But I just can't do that..."

"Mrs. Anderson told me your parents adopted you," Gladys interrupted. "You love them, don't you?"

"Yes, of course I do. Why?"

"Because your baby will love his or her adoptive parents just as much as you love yours."

"But I've always felt different."

"Different? How?"

"It's hard to explain, but I think it's because my brother Frank isn't adopted. If my parents had adopted him, too, I probably wouldn't feel the way I do. I believe my parents treat him better and love him more because he belongs to them. Frank looks exactly like my mother. I don't look like anyone in my family. There have been times when strangers have come up to us and asked my parents where they got the little girl with the dark brown hair. Everyone else in my family has reddish-blond hair."

"I think you're overreacting," Gladys said. "I'm sure your parents love you just as much as they love your brother - perhaps even more. They went to a lot of trouble and expense to get you. It isn't easy to adopt a child. There's usually a long waiting list. I've heard some couples have waited for a baby for seven or eight years." Gladys then asked me if I had always known I was adopted.

"Yes, I've always known," I told her. "When I was a little girl, my parents told me bedtime stories about the special baby they adopted. My father told me often about the very first time he ever saw me. He said that when he stood over my crib and looked down at me, I reached up

61

and grabbed his little finger. According to Dad, that convinced him I was the baby he wanted to take home. Oh, I loved those stories, but that's all they were – stories. I was also told that two years after my brother Frank was born, Mother and Dad had another baby boy who died the very same day. After that, Mother suffered several miscarriages and couldn't have any more children of her own. Ten years later, after having been advised by their minister, Mother and Dad decided to adopt a baby. I've always thought I was second choice."

"But, Sarah, they didn't have to make that choice. They weren't forced into adopting you. Obviously, it was their heartfelt desire to legally adopt you as their daughter. I'm sure they love you very much."

"No, they don't. If they did, they would let me keep my baby. If my baby were related to them, they wouldn't make me give it away."

"It's *because* they love you so much that they're thinking about what's best for your baby."

"But *I'm* the only one who knows what's best for my baby!"

"Have you ever tried to sit down and talk with your mother?"

"No! She won't talk to me. I haven't seen her since the day she appeared at school and embarrassed me about a dress I charged to her account. Oh, how I envy the girls who can talk to their mothers."

14

Against The Rules

Each day that passed brought me closer and closer to my delivery date, and I became more and more frightened.

Meanwhile, even though I had been warned not to become friends with the other girls, I had become fond of the shy, quiet girl named Bonnie who was engaged to be married. She told me the baby she was carrying belonged to her fiancé.

"When I found out I was pregnant," Bonnie said, "I was upset and didn't know what to do. My fiancé, Ted, and I talked it over and decided it would be best for everyone if I came here, had my baby, and placed it for adoption."

"But if you love Ted, how can you give his baby up for adoption?"

"There are times when I feel just awful about it. However, we can't bring ourselves to disgrace our families."

"Are you planning to see your baby?"

"No, if I did, I wouldn't be able to walk away and leave my baby. Ted has assured me we're doing the right thing, and I agree with him."

Although I thought Bonnie was making a terrible mistake, I respected her decision and didn't argue.

Three days later, a day I shall always remember, I awoke with a start. Glancing at the clock, I noted it was only five-thirty in the morning. I made a trip to the bathroom, and when I returned, I pulled the covers up over my head and tried to go back to sleep, but I couldn't. I felt as if I had to go to the bathroom again. To get any relief from the pressure on my abdomen, I sat up and hung my legs over the side of the bed. Kathy heard me moving around and asked me what was wrong.

"I'm not sure."

"Well, go back to sleep."

"I can't. Every time I move, there's a little puddle on my bed sheet, and I have a horrible stomach ache."

"Oh, you silly goose!" Kathy said as she leaned on her elbow and laughed at me. "Your water broke. You're going to have your baby today."

"Oh, Lord! What do I do now?"

"Try to keep calm."

"I can't."

"Yes, you can. I'll go down the hall and get Gladys. Everything's going to be all right."

"I want to call my mother first," I told her. I knew most of the girls had their mothers with them when they went into labor. Some of the mothers traveled thousands of miles to be with their daughters. Because I was panicky, I, too, wanted my mother. At the moment, the fear of childbirth far outweighed the fear I had of her.

Taking a deep breath, I held onto my stomach and slowly walked down the long flight of stairs to the first floor. When I got there, I trembled as I dropped a nickel into the pay telephone. Then I waited. The phone rang once, twice, three times - and on the fourth ring, I heard my mother say, "Hello?"

I could tell by the sound of her voice that I had awakened her from a deep sleep. I inhaled and murmured softly, "Mother, it's me - Sarah. My water broke. I'm scared. Please, Mother, will you come...?"

The silence seemed to last forever. Then I heard the dial tone. My mother had hung up the telephone on me! Standing alone in the dark hallway, I shivered. I replaced the receiver and stared at the phone. Then I heard a familiar voice asking, "Sarah, are you all right?"

"No, Gladys, I'm not all right. My water broke. I'm going to have my baby any second now..."

"Don't worry, dear, it will be awhile yet," she assured me.

"Oh, Gladys, I'm so scared!"

"I know, dear," she said, putting her arm around me and giving me a hug. "I'll help you upstairs to the labor room."

When Gladys mentioned the labor room, I became even more agitated. Pointing my finger at the phone, I blurted out, "She hung up on me! She didn't say a word - she just hung up! I'll never forgive her! I hate my mother!"

"Don't worry about your mother now. You have other things to think about," Gladys said. She helped me climb one step after another toward the third floor which housed the labor rooms, the delivery rooms, and the hospital rooms. By the time we got there, I was gasping for air. I doubled over, clutched my abdomen, and had my first labor pain.

"No one told me labor pains would be anything like this!"

Gladys took me into a small, antiseptic-smelling room and helped me lie down. When the next pain came, I held onto the rail that surrounded the bed. I held on so tightly that my hands hurt. Losing control, I screamed.

"Hush, dear, and try to relax."

"I *can't* relax!"

"You *must*," she said. She told me she was off duty and would stay with me so I wouldn't be alone. She wiped my forehead with a cool, damp cloth. Between labor pains, which were coming more and more frequently, each worse than the last, she held onto my hand and spoke encouragingly to me.

"Have you called my doctor?" I asked. My parents had hired a private physician instead of relying on one of the staff doctors, and I knew I would feel better if he were there.

"Yes, I notified him," Gladys assured me. "But there isn't anything he could do now. You haven't dilated enough. It will probably be an hour or so before you deliver your baby."

But I can't stand this pain. Oh-h-h-h-h-h-h! I hate Mike!"

"Sarah, don't fret. You're doing just fine. It won't be much longer now," Gladys said. But when another hour passed, and I suffered labor pains I thought I couldn't endure, I became hysterical.

Finally, my doctor arrived and examined me. A few minutes later, he moved me into the delivery room, and a mask was placed over my face. I took in the deepest breaths possible so that I could get temporary relief from the hellish pain. When the mask was removed, I suffered the torturous pain of childbirth again.

"I'll never, never let another man touch me!" I screamed. "It's just not worth it!"

Ignoring my outbursts, the doctor instructed me to breathe, not push. But I kept pushing. I begged for more ether. When I thought I couldn't tolerate another moment of pain, the doctor told me to push as hard as I could.

At precisely three-forty that afternoon, March 22, 1949, I heard my baby cry.

"Sarah, you have a little girl," Gladys whispered.

"Is she all right?"

"Yes, dear, she's fine."

"Does she have all her little fingers and toes?"

"Yes, dear."

"I want to see her."

"I'm sorry," the doctor said. "You can't see your baby - it's against the rules."

"Well, I don't give a damn about the rules! Let me see my baby!"

"You *can't* see her," the doctor said again, this time speaking with authority.

"Didn't anyone tell you I'm keeping my baby? You have no right to keep me from seeing her. Who do you think you are, God?"

"Sarah, don't make yourself emotionally ill," Gladys cautioned.

"But, Gladys, she's *my* baby! I want to see her!"

From the expression I saw on Gladys' face, I believe she knew I was suffering more pain now than I had suffered during childbirth.

I struggled to pull myself to a sitting position so that I could see my baby, but the nurse who had assisted the doctor took her away.

I covered my face with both hands. I cried.

15

What's Best For Baby

A pungent aroma of bacon and eggs saturated the air. Clutching my stomach, I vomited profusely.

"Please get that food out of my sight," I pleaded. "I'm sick. I can't eat a thing."

Without arguing, the nurse's aid put the breakfast tray down outside my door. After she changed my bed, she left.

I closed my eyes and welcomed sleep. When I awoke later it was dark outside. Did I sleep all day? Did I have my baby or was it just a dream? Then I saw Gladys standing at the foot of the bed. She was smiling at me.

"I've been waiting for you to awaken," she said. "Tell me, how do you feel?"

"I feel horrible. I have a headache and my stomach's upset."

"Well, dear, you're nauseated because of the large amount of ether you were given, but you'll feel better soon."

"Then it wasn't a dream? I had my baby?"

"Yes, Sarah, you're in a hospital room. You had a baby girl. It's all over now."

I put my hands palm side down on my stomach. It was flat. A part of me that I had loved and nourished for nine months was gone. I felt hollow inside. The empty feeling hurt.

I wanted to get out of bed and run down the hall to the nursery to see my baby. I wanted to hold her, but I realized I wouldn't be allowed into the nursery. I remembered the sound of my baby's first cry and knew, even then, the memory would haunt me forever and ever. Salty tears trickled down my face.

Gladys held my hand. Although she didn't say a word, I appreciated her presence.

When I regained my composure, I looked directly at Gladys and asked, "Is my baby healthy?"

"Yes, she's as healthy as she can be. And she's a beautiful baby."

I bowed my head, closed my eyes and prayed, "Thank you, God."

A moment of serenity and silent prayer followed. Then I thought about my mother and father.

"Have my parents seen my baby?" I asked.

"No, not yet. However, they called to inquire about you and the baby. They're concerned about you. They love you..."

"Don't waste your breath telling me my parents love me. Did you forget that my mother hung up the telephone on me? I hate her!"

"Sarah, you should be ashamed of yourself. I know you don't hate your mother."

"Oh, but I do!"

"I believe you love your mother very much, and you should realize this entire experience has been difficult for her, too."

"How could you feel sorry for her? I think she's a terrible mother!"

"You have no idea what she's been living through. Try to put yourself in her place. She hung up on you because she probably couldn't find the right words to explain exactly how she felt. I think your mother wanted to be here with you when you went into labor, but she couldn't make herself come."

"But, Gladys, you don't even *know* my mother."

"You're right, I don't know her, but I'm a mother. I know how I'd feel if something like this happened to one of my daughters."

"I didn't know you had children."

"I'm a widow with two grown daughters - two adopted daughters."

"Why didn't you tell me?"

"Until now," Gladys explained, "there was no need to mention it. But since I'm an adoptive parent, I think I understand how your mother must feel. My heart goes out to her. It's a shame you can't communicate with one another. It would be better if the two of you could sit down and talk."

"Huh, that's a laugh! My mother won't listen to me. She talks to me, but I can't say a word to her. My grandmother's the only one in my family who ever listens to me. Grandmother has time for me. She treats me like a human being. When she found out I was going to have a baby, she was loving and sympathetic. She said she would always love me no matter what. I wish my mother were more like her."

"Grandmothers are usually more understanding and patient than mothers," Gladys said thoughtfully. "Perhaps it's because they've lived longer - perhaps grandmothers are wiser."

"Yes, maybe they are."

Early the following morning, I had an unexpected visitor who introduced herself as Mrs. Browning, the maternity home social worker.

"I'm here to take your personal history," she said as she sat down in a chair and smiled at me.

"What history? I don't know a damn thing about my background.

How could I? I'm adopted!"

"The fact you're adopted makes no difference," she explained politely. "The maternity home needs certain pertinent information about you – your likes and dislikes. We need to know as much as possible about your childhood so that we can place your baby in a suitable home."

"I'm keeping my baby. I won't talk to you."

"You needn't speak to me in that discourteous tone of voice. I'm only doing my job." She then informed me that my parents wanted me to place my baby for adoption, and since I was still a minor, I had no choice in the matter. "Besides, dear," she said, "someday you'll meet a fine young man and you'll marry. Then you can start a family. Meanwhile, you must think about what's best for your baby."

"If I hear that phrase 'what's best for my baby' one more time, I swear I'll throw up! I've heard it *so many times*! Doesn't anyone understand? I don't *want* my baby raised by strangers who could never, ever understand her! It makes me sick just thinking about it! Why should my baby grow up with adoptive parents when she has me? I'm her *mother*! I love her!"

"Love just isn't enough."

"It's the most important thing in the world. No one in the world could love my baby as much as I do. If I place her for adoption, she'll grow up with millions of unanswered questions. She'll probably end up emotionally crippled. She'll be curious about herself all the days of her life. And she'll think I didn't love her enough to keep her. She'll hate me."

"A child needs a normal life with normal parents - a mother and a *father*. Adoptive parents will love her as their very own. Sarah, you of all people should know that."

I realized the social worker wasn't the person with whom I should be arguing. I wanted to talk to my mother so that I could convince her to allow me to keep my baby. I apologized to Mrs. Browning and decided to answer her questions.

"While you were growing up, what were your special interests?"

"Horses have always been a big part of my life. I've ridden in horse shows all over the United States."

"That's interesting," said Mrs. Browning, writing in her notebook. "Is there anything else?"

"Yes. I love music."

"Do you play an instrument?"

"I play the piano. Although I hated to practice, I'm glad my mother insisted I take lessons. I enjoy listening to records, too," I told her. "Whenever I feel down-in-the-dumps, I put on a record and then I feel better. Music, for me, is magic."

Mrs. Browning nodded and continued to write in her notebook. After she took my medical history concerning childhood diseases and injuries, she asked me to tell her about my baby's father.

"I don't want to talk about Mike. I hate him."

"It's important we know something about him: his physical appearance, his interests, his education and..."

"Well," I said, interrupting, "Mike is a tall, good-looking man who is built like an athlete. He has dark hair and blue eyes. He's a talented artist, a college graduate, and comes from a very good family. That's all I'm going to say about him."

"Thank you. That's quite enough," Mrs. Browning said kindly. Then she asked me if I had named my baby. "We need her name for her original birth certificate," she explained.

"Did you forget? I'm not going to give her up. But if you must know, I named her Elizabeth. I named her Elizabeth after my grandmother."

16

Sign Here

Two days later, I heard familiar footsteps. I looked up to see my mother walking into my room. I was thrilled. But I was worried, too.

Without a word, she sat down in a chair by the window. She smoothed her skirt and slowly removed, one finger at a time, her dainty white gloves. After folding them neatly, she put them into her purse. The fragrance of her expensive perfume wafted through the air. I watched in silence, and waited for her to speak.

"Sarah," she said, finally, "you've ruined your life. I had such wonderful plans for you, but you threw them away. But the worst part of all is that no decent man will want to marry a girl who has had a baby out of wedlock. You've ruined your future. You've disgraced our good name."

"Mother, I'm sorry, but I..."

"Don't you dare interrupt me, Sarah," she said as she stood, pulled herself to her full height and paced the floor. She threw her arms into the air, demonstrating her aggravation.

I thought it was out of character for a woman of her grace and social status to behave this way, but I said nothing.

"How could you have *done* this to me? she demanded. "I've given you everything a girl could possibly want, but you obviously don't appreciate it. Honestly, Sarah, sometimes I'm sorry your father and I adopted you!"

Stunned and hurt, I didn't want to believe the scene I had just witnessed. I knew my mother was disappointed in me, but I had not expected such harsh words. Doesn't she know I'm suffering, too, I wondered? The words I had rehearsed stuck in my throat.

Oblivious to what I was going through, she walked toward the door. "I'm going to the nursery to see your baby," she announced.

For an instant, my heart stopped beating. This was the moment I had been waiting for – the moment my mother would first lay eyes on my baby. I was convinced she would change her mind and let me keep my little Elizabeth. Since I had experienced the agony of childbirth, I now considered myself an adult. Therefore I thought there would be a special bond between us that had not existed before - a woman-to-woman closeness.

While waiting anxiously for her return, I watched the door and prayed, "Please, God! Help me!"

Suddenly, the door sprung open. For a moment there was quiet. Then Mother spoke softly. "Sarah, your baby is beautiful. She looks a lot like you did when you were an infant. Oh, what a precious little life..."

"Mother, please don't cry. I knew you'd let me keep my baby. I just knew you would, and I..."

"Stop! Don't say another word!"

"But, Mother..."

"Sarah, I'm sorry. Dad and I cannot allow you to keep your baby."

"Please, Mother, won't you and Dad adopt her?"

"No, Sarah. We're too old. Dad and I can't raise your child. You must place her for adoption."

"Can't we discuss it?"

"There's nothing to discuss." Without another word, my mother grabbed her purse and ran out of the room.

I ran after her, calling out, "Mother! Mother! Please come back!" But she ignored me and kept going.

Later that evening, sick at heart, all I could think about was my baby. I wanted to see her.

Without worrying about possible consequences I hurried down the hall toward the nursery. I knew Gladys was still on duty, but since she wasn't sitting at her desk, I assumed she had gone downstairs to the cafeteria to get a fresh cup of coffee. I stopped once and looked up and down the hall to make certain no one was watching me. When I reached the nursery, I slowly opened the door and peeked inside. Instinctively, I found my last name on my baby's tiny wristband. As I stood over the crib and looked at her, it was difficult to fully comprehend I had actually given birth to this remarkable little human being, who lay sleeping so peacefully.

Without a moment's hesitation, I picked her up and cradled her in my arms. My breasts throbbed painfully as Mother Nature acknowledged the presence of the infant snuggled close to them.

"Oh, Elizabeth, I love you," I whispered.

Without warning then, the door of the nursery opened.

"Sarah, I feel like taking you over my knee and spanking you," Gladys said. "Don't you realize you're only hurting yourself? Now it will be even more difficult for you when you're forced to leave your baby. Why are you deliberately punishing yourself?"

Gladys shook her head disapprovingly and, without apology, took Elizabeth out of my arms and returned her to her crib. She then took my hand, led me from the nursery to my room down the hall, and helped me into bed.

I thought about my baby and imagined I could feel the warmth of her little body close to mine. Tears streamed down my face. It was hours before I surrendered to sleep.

Early the next afternoon, I was summoned to Mrs. Anderson's office. When I arrived there, she was sitting behind her desk. Directly in front of her desk were two straight-backed chairs, one of which was occupied by my mother.

"Mother, what are you doing here?" I questioned.

Before she could answer, Mrs. Anderson asked me to sit down. "Sarah," she said, "I've called you here to sign the relinquishment paper, or the 'Consent to Adoption' paper as it is legally called...."

"I don't understand."

"Well, my dear," Mrs. Anderson went on to explain, "the baby's mother is required by law to sign a legal document giving her consent for her baby to be placed for adoption. When you sign this paper, you agree in writing to give up all legal right or claim to your child, and you..."

"I won't sign any such paper. I won't give my baby away. For God's sake, Mother, help me!"

"Sarah, you must sign the paper."

"No! I won't! I love my baby - she's part of me. If I lose her, I'll die! You're a woman - you must know how I feel. If not, you're just not human!"

I watched my mother open her purse and take out a lace-trimmed handkerchief. Wiping tears from her eyes, she said softly, "Sarah, I, too, love your baby. Your father and I have discussed raising her. We've given this matter much careful thought. We've prayed about it. Believe me, Sarah, this has been the most difficult decision your father and I have ever made in our lives, but it's settled. We can *not* raise your baby. We're doing what we think is best for you and for her."

"*Please*, Mother! Won't you reconsider?"

"No. The decision has been made. If you don't sign the relinquishment paper, I'll sign it for you," she said, picking up a pen and handing it to me. "Here, Sarah, sign your name."

Robot-like, I took the pen from my mother's outstretched hand. I looked at her. She looked away. Then I signed my name. Shoving my chair away from the desk, I ran out of the room screaming, "No one is going to take my baby away from me!"

I ran up the stairs and headed toward the nursery to get my baby and run away with her. I had no idea where I was going to run, but I was going somewhere.

Then I collapsed and fell to the floor. There was blood everywhere - I was lying in a puddle of blood. "Help me! Someone please help me!" I cried out.

Two nurses and one of the staff doctors lifted me onto a gurney and wheeled me into the emergency room, where I was given several shots. Later when I awoke, I felt as if my mouth were stuffed with cotton. "What happened?" I asked.

Gladys appeared and told me I had hemorrhaged. She also told me I had lost a lot of blood and would be bedridden for three or four days.

"But what if I want to go to the bathroom?" I asked.

"I'll get you a bedpan."

"I won't use a bedpan!"

"If you don't do as you are told and stay off your feet, you'll hemorrhage again," she warned.

When I heard there was a possibility I would hemorrhage again, I knew I couldn't risk running away with my baby.

I felt as if my life were over. Part of me wanted to die.

17

No Decent Man

The next three weeks seemed more like three years. This was, indeed, a black chapter in my life.

Then one day, Gladys walked into my room and announced, "Sarah, you're going home. Your father will be here soon."

"I'm going home?"

I was torn between joy and sadness. I wanted to go home, but I didn't want to leave my baby.

I knew the day the girls left the maternity home, they were allowed to see their babies. I also knew that the majority of them chose not to put themselves through what could be a heartbreaking experience. Yet I was determined to face the torture of a final farewell.

"Are you sure you want to do this?" asked Gladys, apprehensively.

"Yes. I can't go home until I tell Elizabeth goodbye."

"Well, wait at the end of the hall," Gladys said. "I'll go to the nursery and get her."

Tears filled my eyes as I waited for her. I paced the floor and twisted my hair. When Gladys started down the hall with Elizabeth in her arms, I ran to them.

"I want to hold my baby," I said.

"No, Sarah, it's against the rules. All you can do is look at her."

"Oh, Gladys, please let me hold Elizabeth! Please!"

"I should have my head examined," she said. "But it's difficult for me to say no to you." Without further argument, she gently put my baby into my outstretched arms.

Tears seeped from the corners of my eyes as I gazed down at Elizabeth. I held her close. I hugged her. Then I kissed her pedal-soft cheek. "Elizabeth," I murmured, "I won't be around to see you grow up. So I'm placing you into God's hands. I've asked Him to watch over you, and I pray He will give you a good life." I bent and kissed her again. Then before I realized what was happening, Gladys took her out of my arms and whisked her away to the nursery. My baby was gone.

When Gladys returned, she found me standing alone at the end of the hall, crying.

"Sarah," she said, "you're doing the right thing. I know it's difficult for you now, but you've made the right decision to place your baby for adoption."

"But it wasn't my decision," I sobbed.

"Regardless, you're doing the right thing..."

"Whether it's right or wrong," I cried out, interrupting, "I'm sick inside. I feel like I've lost an arm or a leg. I couldn't feel worse if someone I loved just died."

"You'll feel better soon."

"No, I'll always feel the way I feel today."

Deliberately changing the subject, Gladys told me she was going to miss me.

"But we'll stay in touch?"

"No, dear, that wouldn't be wise. Over the years," Gladys explained, "I've tried to make it a strict rule not to get personally involved with the girls who come here. However, in your case, Sarah, I'm afraid I broke that rule, and I've become very fond of you. Yet...I must tell you goodbye. It's time for you to get on with the rest of your life. It's time for you to forget about the past. Believe me, it's better this way. I won't forget you. You'll forever be in my prayers."

"Gladys, we're friends. I love you. I can't lose you, too."

Gladys smiled sweetly. She hugged me, then turned and walked away. I knew I would never see her again.

Suddenly, I felt the warmth of someone's hand in mine. Glancing up, my eyes met the kind, gentle eyes of my father.

"Sarah, I've been searching everywhere for you," he said. "I've come to take you home."

Each time we drove over the smallest bump in the road, I experienced excruciating pain, but I said nothing about it. Instead, I asked my father why he hadn't come to the maternity home to see me or, more importantly, to see my baby.

"I couldn't come," he said bluntly, "I would have been tempted to let you keep your baby. However, Sarah, I wholeheartedly agree with your mother's decision to place her for adoption. It's the right thing to do. And when we get home," he added, "you must not, under any circumstances, talk about your baby. It would be too hard on your mother. Do I make myself clear?"

"Yes, Dad."

By the time we drove up in front of our house, I was doubled over in pain. I told my father I wasn't sure I could walk.

"Don't worry," he said, "I'll carry you just like I used to do when you were a little girl." He swooped me up into his strong arms and carried me into the house, up the stairs to my bedroom, and gently laid me down on the bed. Moments later, Mother walked into the room.

"Welcome home, Sarah," she said. She told me I looked tired and asked if I were all right.

"I have cramps," I told her.

"Well, lie still and rest. You'll feel better after you rest."

"But I want to see Grandmother. Is she in her room?"

The color drained from Mother's face. Turning, she looked out the window.

"Where's my grandmother?" I asked again.

Slowly my mother faced me and said, "Sarah, I'm sorry to have to tell you that your grandmother died three weeks ago."

I gasped and stared at Mother in disbelief. I got up and ran down the hall to my grandmother's bedroom and flung open the door. The room was empty. My grandmother was gone.

"Oh, why is God punishing me?" I screamed. I wanted to cry, but tears wouldn't come. Had I cried so much for my baby that I didn't have any tears left to cry for my grandmother, I wondered? I gazed into the empty room and detected the faint, sweet-smelling bouquet of my grandmother's face powder - the only trace of her that lingered.

Finally, I shut the door behind me and returned to my room. I threw myself on the bed and stared at the ceiling.

Later that evening, Mother appeared and announced, "Sarah, your father and I are going out to dinner. Hettie will bring you a tray and if you need anything, just ring this bell," she added as she placed a silver bell on the night stand.

"Mother, please don't leave me. I'm sick, and I..."

Before I could finish my sentence, blood had soaked my gown and bedclothes. I saw blood dripping down onto the carpet.

"Oh my Lord, Sarah, lie still," Mother instructed. Then she telephoned the doctor.

A short time later the doorbell rang, and Mother ran downstairs to answer it. I heard her say in a loud, angry voice, "No, you can't see my daughter. Sarah is ill. She can't see anyone."

The next voice I heard was my doctor's as he politely introduced himself. Although my parents had hired him, they had never met him. Because he was young and good-looking, he obviously wasn't what my mother had expected.

Hurriedly, she apologized for her faux pas and escorted the doctor up the stairs to my bedroom. He gave me two shots – one to stop the hemorrhaging and one to make me sleep.

Confined to my bed for the next three weeks, I had time to think. I thought about my baby and wondered if someone had adopted her. When my curiosity got the better of me, I telephoned Mrs. Anderson. She informed me my baby had been adopted by a couple who would give her a good life. Knowing Elizabeth was gone, I tried to come to terms with it, but I couldn't. I knew her life had officially begun with parents who would love her, but when I thought about my baby being raised as someone's adopted daughter, I knew the heavy burden of guilt for having left her would haunt me the rest of my life. My spirits sank to an all-time low.

While I recuperated, my parents remained loving and kind. However, when my strength returned, the conflict between my mother and me began all over again. She insisted I return to college.

"I don't feel like a college student," I argued. "I could never go back..."

"Well, you could transfer to another school."

"No, Mother, I won't go, and nothing you say can change my mind." I was thinking less of myself than ever before and had fallen into a trap of self-pity. After all, from my mother's point of view, I had ruined my life.

"Someday, young lady," she said sternly, "you're going to regret that decision."

No, Mother, I won't. But I'll always regret placing my baby for adoption."

It was my father who settled the argument concerning my future by suggesting I attend business college. I enrolled in Miss Hooley's Business School October 5, 1949.

A short time later, I married Tony, a rugged-looking young man with large tattoos on his arms. He wasn't the type of husband I wanted, but my mother's words, "No decent man will want to marry a girl who has had a baby out of wedlock" rang in my ears. With the pain of childbirth long forgotten, I wanted another baby - a baby I could keep.

Rebecca (I call her Becca) was born July 21, 1953. Four years later, my marriage ended in divorce, which came as no surprise to anyone.

The years passed quickly. Becca grew up, married and started a life of her own.

I married a man named Tyler, an older man who reminded me of my father. I felt safe and comfortable with Tyler and realized finally that the love I once had for Mike had been a foolish romantic fantasy – not love at all.

Then I started thinking about my lost baby. I thought about my own birth mother, too, and decided to search for the two of them. However, my father got sick and, following a short illness, died. Devastated by his death, I forgot about searching for my family ties.

A year later, Mother became ill and was hospitalized. After suffering a severe stroke, she motioned for me to come closer.

Slowly, I bent over her bed and listened as she whispered softly, "Sarah, I love you."

The words I had longed to hear for what seemed a lifetime were my mother's last words.

18

Two Needles
in a Haystack

fter my mother's funeral when the sympathy cards stopped coming and friends no longer telephoned to convey their condolences, I felt lost and sad. I resented my parents for dying. I had missed my father terribly after his death, but had consoled myself with the fact that my mother was still living. She needed me, I thought. Now they were both dead and I felt abandoned. Because I was adopted, I believed I had lost the only identity I had ever had.

Once again, I thought about searching for my birth family – my real mother and the baby girl I had, so many years before, reluctantly relinquished for adoption. But then my mother-in-law, an eighty-four year old widow in failing health, came to live with us.

Anna (I called her "Mother") was a tiny woman who reminded me of my grandmother. As Anna grew older and more frail, she relied on me for her baths, meals, daily medication, and transportation to and from the doctor's office and the beauty shop. I became very fond of her. She made me feel needed. Five and a half years later when she died, it was like losing a child. The world looked gray, and I fell into a deep depression again.

One evening, quite unexpectedly, Tyler said, "Sarah, why don't you search for your real mother and your baby?"

"Well, I haven't thought about it lately," I told him. I believed his suggestion was a good one, but the only problem was I didn't know where to begin.

I remembered that after my father died, I had found a briefcase stuck in the back of his closet. The briefcase contained an old yellowed-with-age "Petition For Control and Custody of Child". I knew the child was me. From the document, I learned my birth mother's maiden name and the name she had given me – Marilyn. The names of my

79

adoptive parents were listed as the petitioners for my adoption. The maternity home where I had been born, which, to my surprise, was located in the city where I lived, was named as the custodian of the child. There was also a hand-written letter that had been sent to my parents from the administrator of the home. She had described my real mother as a sweet, even-tempered young woman named Marie. Marie, according to the letter, had been a twenty-two-year-old college student who had intended to return to school after the birth of her baby. The administrator went on to describe Marie as an attractive young woman with dark hair and hazel eyes. She was a delightful girl who had come from a very good family and was a good student with special interests that included music and sports.

Although the information concerning Marie was limited, I believed I had enough material to initiate a search. I had decided to search for her first, since she, according to the letter, was now seventy-eight years old.

That night when I told Tyler I didn't know where to begin searching, he suggested I get in touch with the maternity home administrator who had written the letter to my parents.

"Do you think she's still living?"

"Probably."

When I looked in the telephone book, I found fourteen Jordons, but no Irene Jordon. Determined to find her, I dialed the first Jordon listed. When a woman answered, I asked to speak to Irene.

"I'm sorry," she said, "you have the wrong number."

Eleven calls later, a woman answered who said, "This is Irene Jordon."

"Are you the woman who was the administrator of the maternity home for unwed mothers which was located on Brookside Road?" I asked.

"Yes, I am, but..."

"I was born there," I said, excitedly. "And I'm searching for my real mother. Can you please help me find her?"

"My dear," said Irene Jordon, "there isn't a day that goes by that I don't get three or four telephone call inquiries from someone like you who is looking for her mother or her baby. I'll tell you what I tell everyone else. No, I can't help you. All the adoption records are sealed. It would be against the law to give you any information, and even if I could, I wouldn't. Too many lives would be affected. Too many people could get hurt."

"I have no intention of hurting anyone," I argued, "Can't you tell me if you remember my mother? She was there in the spring of 1932. Her name was Marie...."

"My dear girl," said Mrs. Jordon, "I'm doing well to remember my own name. I'm an eighty-four-year-old woman who spent forty seven of those years as the administrator of one of the most prestigious maternity homes for unwed mothers in the entire country. Over the years, hundreds and hundreds of girls, all of whom were from prominent families, came and went. And you expect me to remember your mother? Well! I never!"

"I thought there was a chance you might remember her," I said almost apologetically. I realized then, even though I had talked with Mrs. Jordon for a short time, she was obviously opposed to my search. I believed she knew a lot more than she was willing to tell me. I was disappointed. Explaining that it was very important for me to find my real mother, I told Mrs. Jordon I wouldn't give up until I located her.

"Well, my dear, if God wants you to find her, you will, but if not, no matter what you do, you won't. You should understand you could get hurt, and your family could get hurt, too. But if you're determined to find her, I can tell you about a search and support group for adult adoptees and birthparents. The organization conducts training programs and seminars to teach people how to search. And there's also a reunion registry available that...."

"How do I get in touch with them?" I interrupted.

"I'll give you the telephone number of a woman named Joan Banner, who is the president and research director for the group. If anyone can help you, Joan can."

After thanking Mrs. Jordon, I telephoned Joan Banner. She invited Tyler and me to attend the next meeting of the search and support group to be held the following Saturday morning at the main library building.

February 22, 1986 - a day that will remain in my memory forever - is the day I started my search.

When the elevator door opened, Tyler and I stepped out on the seventh floor of the main library building. Our footsteps echoed as we hurried down the long corridor and headed toward a room at the end of the hall.

Enthusiastically, I walked into the room and sat down at a large conference table. Tyler pulled out a chair and sat next to me. Then our presence was acknowledged by Joan Banner, who shook hands with us and welcomed us to the group.

Scrutinizing the room, I saw twenty-five or thirty people of all ages - men and women who were obviously there to search for someone – a parent, child, or perhaps a sibling. I studied their faces and hoped I would find someone who looked like my real mother or my relinquished daughter, but no one fit the vivid description I had carried in my mind all these years. Although I was disappointed, I listened as the members of the group took turns explaining why they were there and for whom they were searching.

A man who looked to be in his late seventies stood and told the group he had learned only recently that his parents had adopted him. "The day my mother died," he said, "she told me I was adopted. She lied to me all those years. I'm not the person I thought I was. I don't know who I am, and I feel like I'm drowning."

"You've had a terrible shock," Joan said sympathetically.

"Yes, I'm shocked, but I'm angry, too. My parents should have told me I was adopted. I had a right to know. And I should have been given an opportunity to search for my birthparents, but now it's too late. Undoubtedly they're no longer living. I came here hoping to find a half-brother or a half-sister. Hoping to find someone..."

"I'll put you in touch with Mr. Henry," Joan said. "He specializes in helping people find siblings. If you like, I'll ask him to be your sponsor. I'm sure he'll be able to help you. It won't be long until you feel much better about yourself. You'll see."

The man poured out his thanks to Joan. Then he took a handkerchief from his pocket and wiped tears from his eyes. A stillness settled over the room. There was an unspoken camaraderie evident in the eyes of the others. They were deeply concerned about this man.

Then the mood changed. An attractive woman stood up. Smiling, she told the group she had found and had been reunited with her real mother. The announcement met with loud clapping and congratulations.

"Did your reunion go well?" Joan asked.

"Yes, very well," she answered. "We had a wonderful time getting acquainted with one another." She opened her purse, removed several snapshots, and passed them around the table for everyone to see.

I wondered what it would feel like to meet the person or, in my case, the two people I was searching for. I smiled as I pondered the possibility of it. Down deep in my heart, however, I was not optimistic. I believed it would be like looking for the proverbial needle in the haystack. Like *two* needles in a haystack! But I continued to listen with interest as the other members of the group reported the progress they were making in their searches. Suddenly, all eyes were on me. It was my turn to speak.

I stood up. Clearing my throat, I said, "I'm here to search for my real mother and my baby girl I placed for adoption thirty three years ago." A sharp twinge of guilt and embarrassment tugged at my heart when I confessed publicly that I had had a baby out of wedlock. A kind-looking middle aged woman sitting across the table from me seemed to sense my dilemma.

"Don't be embarrassed, dear," she said, smiling sweetly. "We're all here to search for someone. And we're here to give each other support and encouragement. I, too, am adopted and placed a baby for adoption. I've been told it isn't uncommon for those of us who are adopted to have a baby out of wedlock. There's something buried deep within us that prompts us to want to be truly related to someone else. We want to feel connected to another human being."

"That's right," Joan agreed. Then she added, diplomatically, "We don't use the term 'real mother' or 'my baby'. Instead, we say 'birthmother', 'birth son' or 'birth daughter'. And we always refer to our adoptive parents simply as our parents. It's much less confusing that way."

"I'm sorry. I didn't know." Then quickly changing the subject, I told Joan I was planning to search for my birthmother first.

"If I were you," she said, "I'd search for my birth daughter first. Her adoption took place more recently. However, whomever you choose to look for first, it's important that you know you're about to begin the most traumatic, emotional experience of your entire life. Conducting a search can create numerous incomprehensible problems. And you should prepare yourself for possible rejection."

"I wouldn't be here if I weren't determined. I know there's a possibility of rejection, but I just have to search. It's something I've thought about all my life. Where do I start?"

"Well, the first thing you should do," Joan instructed, "is fill out two registration forms - one for your birth daughter and one for your birthmother. You can take them home, and after you've filled them out, make two copies. One copy will be placed in our reunion registry and the other will be mailed to the International Soundex Reunion Registry in Carson City, Nevada. It is a centralized registry that is open to all adult adoptees and birthparents."

Thanking Joan, I stuck the registration forms into my purse.

Before Tyler and I left the meeting that day, Joan graciously offered to be my sponsor. I was encouraged. I prayed I would be successful in locating these two women who meant so much to me.

19

Waiting (Im)patiently

After the registration forms had been carefully filled out, copied and mailed, I called Joan and asked her what I should do next.

"Well, she said, "you should write a query letter to the Judge of the Juvenile Court where you were adopted and a similar letter to the judge where your birth daughter was adopted."

"We were both adopted from the same court," I told her.

"That's very unusual, but it will make your search a lot easier because you'll be dealing with only one judge. You should write to him immediately before he leaves to sit on the bench of another court. This particular judge cooperates with birth parents and adoptees, but unfortunately most judges don't. When you write to him," Joan went on, "give him all the information you have about your birth daughter: her birth name, the name and address of the maternity home where she was born and the date of her birth. Ask the judge to send you any non-identifying information he has in her file. And it wouldn't be a bad idea if you told him you and your husband were preparing a will and wanted to include your birth daughter."

"I've thought often about leaving Elizabeth something," I said. "I think I owe her that much..."

"No, Sarah, legally you don't owe her a thing. But if you feel morally obligated to leave her one or two items, the judge will probably attempt to locate her. And, Sarah, you should write him a similar query letter concerning your birth mother and include any information you have about her. After you've written the letters, have them notarized. Oh, and one more thing," said Joan, "You should telephone the search and support group's coordinating secretary and place an ad in our quarterly newsletter."

"What do I owe you for all your help?" I asked.

"I never accept even the smallest token gift."

"You donate your time?"

"Yes, Sarah, I enjoy helping people."

When I finished writing the query letters to the Judge of Juvenile Court, I took them to the library, made copies and hurried to the bank to have them notarized. After mailing them, I returned home and telephoned the coordinating secretary as Joan had instructed. Then the waiting began.

Each day that passed seemed like an eternity.

Tyler and I continued to attend the monthly meetings of the search and support group. When the meetings were over, I was usually encouraged. And I waited as patiently as I knew how to hear from the judge. After two and a half months passed and I had not heard from him, I started worrying.

"It often takes three or four months to receive a reply from the judge," Joan told me. "But don't get discouraged. I assure you, he will answer your queries."

Three weeks and two days later, as Joan had predicted, I received the replies from the judge. Nervously tearing open the first letter, I sat down and read:

Dear Ms. Sarah Smith:

The only information in the court file concerning your birth parents is a Consent to Adoption form signed by your birth mother, a copy of which I enclose.

The court file reflects that your adoptive parents applied at a maternity home for an adopted child. However, that home has not been in operation for a number of years. If any social or medical history of your birth parents was obtained, it would have been obtained by that agency and that information was not turned over to this court. I have absolutely no information as to the present location or any report concerning your birth parents or if, in fact, that information was ever accumulated.

I have been advised by a court employee who worked as a liaison worker for the home at the time it ceased operation twenty years ago, that all the records of that institution were destroyed by fire approximately fifteen years ago. I am sorry I could not provide you with further information.

Yours truly,
Judge William D. Jason

Well, I had not expected to receive such discouraging news.

For years I had dreamed about finding my birth mother. Now that dream seemed impossible. I was close to tears as I picked up the relinquishment paper my birth mother had signed.

Placing my forefinger over her signature, I attempted to create a bond between her and me. I remembered then that Joan had warned me that it would be difficult to find her, since my adoption had taken place so many years ago. When I looked at the relinquishment paper again, I tried to imagine what she - a young woman named Marie - must have gone through the day she had signed her baby away. Because I had gone through an identical, devastating experience myself, my heart ached for her.

I shrugged as I told myself I would not give up the search for the woman - the stranger - who had given me the gift of life. Over the years, I had allowed the desire to find her to become more than an obsession - it had become a deadly cancer in my mind. But of course no one had suspected how I felt.

Concealing my emotions, I opened the other letter from the judge and read:

Dear Ms. Sarah Smith:

> *If you desire to make a will bequeathing part or all of your estate to the daughter that you placed for adoption through this court in March, 1949, I would suggest that you make that bequest to the female child born March 22, 1949, and named Elizabeth. Send that document to me and I will attempt to locate the adoptive parents and the adoptive child, and forward your testamentary document to them.*

> *I am enclosing a photocopy of the Consent to Adoption of child which you signed March 30, 1949.*

> *Yours truly,*
> *Judge William D. Jason*

Tears moistened my face. I remembered that horrible day, so long ago, when I had signed my name to that document which had changed Elizabeth's and my lives forever. I couldn't help but think about what "could have been", and the guilt for having relinquished my baby came back to haunt me.

Suddenly, I noticed the names of my birth daughter's adoptive parents, hand-written on the upper left-hand corner of the Consent to Adoption paper. I could read their first names, but couldn't make out their last name. Rushing to the desk, I opened a drawer and pulled out a magnifying glass. It didn't help.

When Tyler came home later that evening, he, too, attempted to make out their last name, but soon announced it was illegible.

I was devastated. If I knew the name of the couple who had adopted Elizabeth, I believed I could find her. I hoped she lived nearby, perhaps as close as the next block.

Sensing my frustration, Tyler suggested I telephone Joan.

"She doesn't take any calls from the members of the search and support group on weekends," I told him. "I'll call her the first thing Monday morning."

20

Say Hello!

E arly Monday morning, I telephoned Joan and explained my predicament. She told me to calm down, first. Then she asked if I wanted her to take a look at the Consent to Adoption paper.

"Over the years," she said, "I've looked at so many similar legal documents that perhaps I can make out their last name."

With enthusiasm, I accepted Joan's offer.

That afternoon when we met at the mall, I took the document out of my purse and handed it to Joan. I stood back, watching and waiting.

Without a word, Joan studied the document for only a few minutes. She wrote a name on a piece of paper, smiled and handed it to me.

"What do you know that I don't know?" I questioned. But I had learned a long time ago never to question Joan about her source of information. Consequently, I thanked her for her help and announced, "I'm going home and look up their name in the telephone book, and..."

"No, Sarah, don't do that."

"Why not?"

"Because your birth daughter probably doesn't live around here," Joan said emphatically. "Besides, you could do far more harm than good. Our search and support group has over 500 sister support groups located in cities throughout the United States. These groups exchange information. For instance, if a person lives in San Francisco, was born in Kansas City and has a birth mother who lives in Minneapolis, the networks contact each other for assistance."

"But I can't just sit around doing nothing."

"When you get home, you can write a letter waiving your right of confidentiality, and be sure to have the letter notarized. Send it to the judge of the juvenile court and request that it be placed in your birth daughter's file."

"What else can I do?"

"Nothing! All you can do now is wait."

Conducting a search was much harder, more time consuming and more emotional than I had anticipated. During the first few days that had turned slowly into weeks, I had learned a certain amount of patience, yet had never developed the habit of it. I was certain Joan was aware of my inability to sit quietly and wait.

Acknowledging this, Joan smiled and put her arm around my shoulder. "Sarah," she said, "if it will make you feel any better, I'm sure you won't have to wait much longer."

Encouraged, I returned home, sat down at my desk and wrote the letter to the judge as Joan had advised.

During the weeks that followed, Tyler and I continued to attend the monthly meetings of the search and support group. The elderly gentleman who was searching for a sibling was still searching. He told everyone he would search forever until he was successful in locating someone to whom he was biologically related.

The woman who was adopted and looking for her birth mother as well as her relinquished son had found her birth mother. Unfortunately, her birth mother wanted nothing to do with her, since she had married and made a new life for herself which did not include the baby she had placed for adoption. Joan told the woman there was a chance her birth mother would change her mind. "Often it takes awhile for a person to get over the tremendous shock of having been found."

A nice-looking young man I'd never met before was thrilled because he had found an identical twin brother he hadn't known existed. Along with other members of the group, I shared his joy.

I had become good friends with some of the other women in the group. Often we talked on the telephone for hours and compared notes. We gave each other support and "pep talks" whenever we were feeling low. Although I kept busy, the days and especially the nights dragged by ever so slowly.

On Tuesday morning, Joan telephoned me. I didn't think much about it, since I assumed she was calling to lend encouragement as she had done so many times before. But when she asked me how I felt, I became suspicious.

"I feel fine," I told her.

"Are you sitting down?"

"Yes, I'm sitting down. Why?"

"Oh, Sarah, I have the most wonderful news! I found your birth daughter!"

When I recovered from the total shock, which was more severe than I had expected, I murmured, "Are you sure?"

"Yes, I'm positive - everything checks out. For the past five months, I've been in touch with one of our sister support groups in another state. Virginia, the research director of the group, has been successful in locating your birth daughter."

"You've known about this for five months and you didn't tell me?"

"I didn't want to mention it until I was absolutely sure we could find her. I didn't want to get your hopes up..."

"You have no idea what I've been living through," I said, almost yelling. I was torn between anger at Joan for not telling me and the overwhelming gratification at the prospect of meeting my birth daughter. My adrenaline flowed. My rampant emotions startled me. Tears slid down my face. I prayed aloud, "Thank you, God." There was a lump in my throat when I asked, "Have you talked to Elizabeth?"

"Her name is not Elizabeth," Joan proclaimed. "Her adoptive parents named her Jennifer."

"When she was a baby, her name was Elizabeth. But I always knew her name would be changed. Jennifer...Jennifer...well, it's a pretty name."

Suddenly and without warning, I was overcome with panic. "What if she doesn't want to meet me?"

"Oh, but she does! I haven't talked to Jennifer, but I spoke with her husband, Ben, who told me Jennifer tried to find you about four and a half years ago, but she was unsuccessful."

"Well, that makes me feel a lot better," I admitted. Then I asked Joan if she had my birth daughter's telephone number.

"Yes," she answered. "Do you want to call her, or would you prefer to have me act as your intermediary?"

I knew Joan had many years experience as the research director and had acted as an intermediary for many people. I was sure she could handle this delicate situation better than I could; therefore, I accepted her offer. Readily admitting my inadequacy in this matter of such significance, I added, "I wouldn't know exactly what to say. I'd probably cry."

"Well, don't worry. I'll call Jennifer for you. Meanwhile, try to relax. I'll call you back just as soon as I've spoken with her."

Relax! I couldn't relax - who could at a time like this? All I could do was think about my birth daughter. In my heart, she would always be my baby, but I knew only too well that even though we shared a special bond only a mother could share with another human being, still we were strangers. I felt angry about this; then I felt guilty for feeling angry.

While I waited anxiously to hear from Joan, I paced the floor, twisted my hair, and smoked cigarette after cigarette.

Three hours later when the telephone finally rang, I answered it on the first ring.

"Sarah," Joan said, "would you like to speak to your birth daughter?"

"Oh, yes..."

"Well, say hello. This is a three-way conference call. Take a deep breath, open your mouth and say hello."

21

Beautiful & Bittersweet

"**H**ello...Jennifer?"

"Hello," came a timid-sounding voice.

The static on the line made it almost impossible to hear Jennifer, so I asked her to please speak up.

"I'm afraid we have a bad connection," Joan broke in. "I'll hang up now so that Jennifer can call you back."

Nervously, I replaced the receiver. I waited. Seconds later when Jennifer called I could hear her perfectly.

"Are you *really* my mother?" she asked.

"Yes, Jennifer, I'm your birth mother. I have legal documents, including the Consent to Adoption paper, that prove it..."

"Can you give me the name of the doctor who delivered me?" Jennifer asked, politely interrupting.

"Of course; his name was Dr. Robert A. Weederman."

"Where was I born?"

"At the Hillcrest Maternity Home."

"I just wanted to be sure you were the person Joan Banner said you were," explained Jennifer. After a pause, she said, "Thank you for giving me the gift of life."

Touched by her words, I felt tears filling my eyes.

Unaware of the emotion I was experiencing, Jennifer asked me if she had any half-brothers or half-sisters.

"Yes, you have a half-sister, Rebecca, who is married and has three boys. Becca and her family live nearby."

"Does she know about me?"

"Yes, dear. I told her after her first baby was born. I thought she had a right to know and was mature enough to handle it."

"Oh, I've always had a strong feeling that somewhere in the world I had a sister. Would you mind if I called her?"

Willingly, I gave Jennifer Becca's number.

Before we said goodbye, Jennifer promised she would call back the minute she finished talking to Becca.

I had always hoped the girls – one a daughter I had raised and one who had been raised as someone's adopted daughter – would someday be good friends. I wanted Becca to have a sister to feel close to after I died, though I knew I couldn't force them to accept one another. I wondered how Becca would react when she realized Jennifer was a living-breathing person, and not merely someone whom her mother had spoken about often. Engulfed in deep thought, I jumped when the telephone rang. As I had expected, it was Jennifer.

"I had a wonderful conversation with Becca," she said. "I can't wait to meet her. But more importantly, I can't wait to meet you. Would it be all right if Ben and I came for a visit?"

"I thought you'd never ask!"

It was decided that Jennifer and Ben would come the following Friday afternoon and spend the weekend. When I told Jennifer that Tyler and I would be glad to meet them at the airport, she hesitated a moment and then said, "I don't think it would be a good idea if we met in a crowded airport. I'd probably faint and embarrass myself."

"I'd be the one most likely to faint," I confessed. Then I told Jennifer that it was important for all of us to feel comfortable when we met for the very first time.

Agreeing, Jennifer suggested that she and Ben rent a car at the airport and drive to a motel near our house.

"And when we get there," she said, "I'll give you a call so we can meet in the privacy of our motel room, if that's all right with you."

"Yes, dear, that will be fine."

I had waited thirty-some years to meet my birth daughter, yet the three days that followed were undoubtedly the longest days in my life. I deliberately kept busy. I cleaned the cupboards and closets, polished the furniture and woodwork, washed and ironed the curtains, vacuumed the carpets and drapes, and shined the brass and silver, but still the time dragged by slowly. When Friday finally came, everything was under control except my shaky emotions.

Excited, I got out of bed early Friday morning and hurried downstairs. I expected to see Tyler, but he wasn't there. I found a note in my coffee cup:

Sarah, darling,

When I left early this morning, you were sleeping like a baby, and I didn't have the heart to wake you.

I know this is a very special day in your life. A day you have looked forward to for a long, long time. Until I see you this evening, my thoughts will be with you.

Love, Tyler

I held Tyler's note close to my heart and shivered as I thought about the day ahead of me. After drinking several cups of coffee, I went back upstairs to take a bath.

The sound of the water rushing into the tub had a calming effect. When the tub was almost overflowing, I dumped in sweet-smelling bath salts. Extending a leg, I tested the temperature and slowly lowered myself into the soothing warm water. "Oh, this feels good," I said aloud.

When I finished bathing, I dressed in my new red suit. I stood in front of the full-length mirror and stared at myself. Although the suit was pretty, it just wasn't me. I didn't recognize the stranger in the mirror. Suddenly I felt light-headed. My arms felt numb; my legs like soft putty.

I sat down in the nearest chair, closed my eyes and prayed – "Please, God, don't let me get sick today." Then I heard a voice.

"Mom, are you ready to leave?" asked Becca. Jennifer and Ben had arrived at their hotel. It had been arranged that Becca and I would go together to meet Jennifer and Ben so we could give each other moral support. Becca had graciously offered to drive, believing I would be too nervous to drive myself anywhere.

"But Jennifer said she'd call *me*," I said.

"Well, she's anxious about meeting you, so she telephoned me instead."

"She's not the only one who's anxious," I mouthed as I descended the stairs.

"Oh, Mom, you look beautiful!"

"Thank you, dear, but I don't feel beautiful. I'm frightened, and worried about meeting Jennifer. What if she doesn't like me?"

"I'm sure she'll love you just as much as I do. But, Mom, we have to hurry now. Jennifer's waiting eagerly to meet you."

After Becca put the key into the ignition and started the car, she glanced over at me. "You look pale, Mom. Do you feel all right?"

"No, not really. My new shoes are too small, my suit skirt is too long, my silk blouse is too big and I have a horrible headache."

"Oh, you're just nervous."

"Aren't you?"

"Yes, a little," Becca said as she backed the car out of the drive. She headed down the street and skillfully maneuvered through heavy traffic until we reached the outskirts of town. About twenty minutes later, we drove into the motel parking lot.

As I was getting out of the car, I saw a young couple walking toward us. The young man fit the description Jennifer had given of her husband Ben. Immediately I knew the beautiful young woman with him was my birth daughter.

A whirlwind of feelings raced through my head. I shook with anticipation. The late September day was hot and humid. Nervous perspiration appeared on my forehead as I watched the young woman come closer and closer. Moments later, Jennifer and I stood face to face.

"You're my birthmother...?"

Unable to speak, I nodded.

Without a word, she threw her arms around me. A surge of warmth crept over me. Tears rolled down my face and intermingled with Jennifer's. We stood back and looked at one another. We were openly searching for the family resemblance we were hoping to find. Studying Jennifer, I noticed that she was a small person, approximately five foot three inches tall and couldn't weigh more than ninety pounds. She had brown shoulder-length hair and expressive hazel eyes. She had high cheek bones like mine, and a delicate small nose. When she smiled, I saw her beautiful, evenly-shaped white teeth. As I gazed at her, I could see there was, indeed, a family likeness. "She looks exactly like I thought she would," I said to myself. We continued to gaze at each other as if in a trance. We cried. We laughed. We cried again. I thought about Becca. I had momentarily forgotten her since being caught up in the enchantment of this special moment in my life.

I turned to look for her.

"If you're looking for your daughter," Jennifer's husband said, "I saw her go back to the car."

I ran back to the car and found Becca sitting alone in the passenger seat. She looked as if she were about to cry. The sad expression on her face was one I would never forget. She looked like a lost child. Opening the car door, I took her hand in mine as I had done so many times before.

"Come, dear," I said. "Come meet your sister."

Frowning, Becca looked away.

I reached into the car, gently helped her out and looped my arm in hers. Together, we walked to where Jennifer was waiting for us.

Becca and Jennifer smiled at one another. They hugged. They laughed. They stood back and gazed deeply into each other's faces. Although they didn't look a lot alike – Becca's hair was blond, Jennifer's brown – I saw some similarities, the shape of their faces, their eyes and their smiles.

While the sisters were getting acquainted, I took the opportunity to introduce myself to Jennifer's husband Ben. While we were talking, I noticed we were still standing in the middle of the motel parking lot - not the best place to visit. I wondered why Jennifer and Ben had not waited in their motel room as previously planned. This prompted me to say, "Come, girls, let's go home."

When we got into the car and started home, I turned to Jennifer and, because my curiosity was getting the better of me, asked why she hadn't waited in the privacy of the motel room.

"Well, I was going to," she said, " but I was so excited and nervous about meeting you that I couldn't sit still. I remembered you said you would be wearing a red suit, so when I saw you getting out of the car, I knew right away you were my birth mother."

Smiling, I asked her if she and Ben had a good flight.

"Yes, it was fine, with the exception of a little turbulence," Jennifer said.

The next few minutes were a bit awkward for all of us. The impulse to take my birth daughter into my arms and hug her was still there, but there was a stronger impulse – just to stare at her. I couldn't take my eyes off her!

In a desperate attempt to keep the conversation flowing, I asked Jennifer and Ben if they were satisfied with their motel room.

"Yes, it's a nice room," they said in unison.

After weaving in and out of heavy rush-hour traffic, Becca finally drove her car into our driveway and turned off the ignition.

Tyler came rushing out of the house to greet us. Smiling, he shook hands with Ben and kissed Jennifer's cheek. He handed Jennifer a long-stem red rose. Then he gave one to Becca and the last one to me.

"I wanted you girls to have something special so you would always remember this day," he said as he escorted us into the house. He asked everyone to sit down and make themselves comfortable. He then told me he had picked up the fried chicken dinner as I had asked him to do.

I had planned that we would all eat dinner together, including Becca's husband, Tom, and her three boys. But when I looked around, Becca had disappeared. One minute she was there - the next she was gone.

"Why did Becca leave in such a hurry?" Tyler asked.

"I'm not sure," I answered.

In the depths of my mother's intuition, however, I suspected Becca was having difficulty accepting Jennifer.

22

It Would Break
My Mother's Heart

Although I was upset with Becca's refusal to participate in the planned family activities, I was determined not to let anything or anyone ruin the precious moments God had given me to spend with my birth daughter.

When Jennifer, Ben, Tyler and I sat down to eat dinner and I looked across the table at Jennifer, I thought of the old cliche, "somebody pinch me please." It was difficult to realize I was actually sitting in the same room with this lovely young woman - the baby I had given birth to.

At first the conversation was awkward. Neither Jennifer nor I knew what to say to one another. Looking back, I believe we were trying too hard. I was eager to develop a special rapport between us, yet I knew the only relationship I could possibly hope for was friendship - something I'd gladly settle for.

As we continued to visit, I learned, to my surprise, Jennifer and Ben had been in our metropolitan area several times when she had accompanied him on business trips. I had been in the suburb of the large city where Jennifer and Ben lived many times while visiting my aunt and uncle. Unknown to us, we could have rubbed elbows in a shopping mall or a restaurant.

Suspecting Jennifer may have questions she wanted to ask and sensing she was timid, I said I would be happy to answer any question she wanted to ask. I wasn't prepared for the first one, however.

Jennifer turned to me. In a shaky-sounding quiet voice, she asked, "Why did you give me up for adoption?"

I swallowed hard and almost choked on the piece of chicken I was eating. I opened my mouth and closed it, taking in air. Waiting a long moment in an attempt to control myself, I stared at the floor. Finally I looked at her and said, "Jennifer, dear, in the late 1940s, young unmarried women did not keep their babies."

"Why not...?"

"Unfortunately, society frowned on such things."

"Oh...?"

"Yes. I loved you and wanted to keep you. I did everything humanly possible to do so, but my mother insisted I place you for adoption. At the time, and I'm ashamed of it now, I hated her. I hated her even though I knew she was thinking about what was best for both of us. She knew I couldn't give you a good life with advantages and opportunities you deserved, and she..."

"It's impossible for me," Jennifer said, interrupting, "to understand why a woman would give her baby up for adoption." It was then she told me she and Ben had been unable to have children. "And because I was adopted," she explained, "I wanted a baby more than anything else in the world so that I would be truly related to someone. When I found out I couldn't have a baby of my own, I was brokenhearted. I thought my life was over. I didn't want to live. I got sick. Brooding, I stayed in bed for almost a year. It wasn't until I became a born-again Christian that I was able to go on with my life. Two and a half years later, we adopted a baby and named her Elizabeth."

"You named your adopted daughter Elizabeth?"

"Yes, we named her what I had been told you had named me. We call her Beth. She's ten years old now. Our youngest daughter, whom we adopted three years later, is named Doris. We call her Dori."

I was astonished to learn that Jennifer's children were adopted. No wonder she can't comprehend why I placed her for adoption, I thought to myself. I knew any young woman who desperately wanted a baby and couldn't have one could never fathom, even in her wildest dreams, why a woman who had a baby would relinquish it. The anguish I had lived through when I had signed the Consent to Adoption paper rushed through my mind. Painful memories from the past prompted me to quickly change the subject.

"Tell me," I asked, "did you have a happy childhood?"

"Yes, I had a very happy childhood. My parents provided me with everything a little girl could want. They sent me to private schools where I was given a good education along with dancing lessons and piano lessons. I was given all the comforts and necessities of life and then some, yet...there was something missing in my life."

As I listened to Jennifer, I identified with her. I had felt the very same way as a child. Then, because I envied them so, I thought about Jennifer's adoptive parents. (Joan had told me they were still living.) I was curious about them and asked Jennifer if they knew she had come here to meet me.

"No, I chose not to tell them. I was afraid it would break my mother's heart, and I suspected that my father would be terribly hurt and disappointed in me. Ben and I decided it would be better for everyone, including our children, if we kept this trip a secret. I do hope you understand."

"Yes, of course I understand," I told her. "The majority of adoptive parents resent their children's curiosity concerning their birth family ties. The adoptive parents feel threatened."

"Oh, I agree with you," Jennifer said hastily. "I know how threatened I would feel if my adopted daughters decided someday they wanted to meet their birth mothers. It frightens me. And if their birth mothers ever came looking for them, I'd chase them away with a baseball bat."

"Do you love your adoptive parents any less because you wanted to meet me?"

"No, of course not."

"Well, Jennifer," I said, "you should realize those of us who are adopted have two sets of parents, our adoptive parents – the only ones we've ever known and loved - and our birth parents – the ones who gave us life. Any feelings you have for me, don't cancel out the love and respect you will always have for your adoptive parents. And you needn't worry about your children's curiosity concerning their birth parents. Only adult adoptees are allowed to search, unless, of course, there is a medical emergency and even then the information they need is often denied them. So don't borrow trouble."

Long after Ben and Tyler had politely excused themselves from the table, Jennifer and I continued talking. There was so much I wanted to know about her. Time passed quickly. I learned she and Ben lived in a large house out in the country.

"Behind our house," said Jennifer, "is a barn where we stable four saddle horses. I was told that you loved horses and had ridden in many horse shows. I was also told you loved music."

Confirming Jennifer's last statements and realizing it was getting late, Jennifer and I agreed the four of us would meet again the following morning at their motel.

23

Call Me Sarah

Before Tyler and I left the house the next morning to meet Jennifer and Ben for breakfast, I telephoned Becca to see if she wanted to join us. Without giving a reason, she said no. Although I was disappointed, I didn't argue, because I believed she was resentful of the time and attention I was giving Jennifer. Early on, I had suspected she would be, but thought she'd get over it.

When we finished eating breakfast, we got into Tyler's car so we could show Jennifer where she had been born. I reached over and squeezed her hand and, for awhile, time stood still. Then I realized Tyler had pulled to the curb and turned off the ignition.

I looked out the car window and stared at the gray, majestic-looking building that had once been a maternity home for unwed mothers. I hated the word "unwed" and knew most young women of the late 1980s kept their babies born out of wedlock. Envying them, I felt cheated since I was from a generation of women forced by their parents and society to relinquish their babies. As I predicted many years ago, times had changed - for the better.

Continuing to gaze up at the old, obviously empty building, I shivered. Goose bumps appeared on my arms and legs as painful echoes from all my yesterdays came rushing into my head. I noticed, to my surprise, that the twisted old pine tree with its puny branches reaching toward the sky had withstood the passing of the years. The steps I had climbed that day so long ago were littered with scraps of paper and empty beer cans. Remembering the past, I fought to hold back the tears as I pointed to a window on the third floor where Jennifer had been born.

Jennifer's eyes widened as she looked up at the window. I believe she sensed a connection between us; she took my trembling hand in hers and asked, "Did you have a hard delivery?"

"It's difficult to explain," I told her, "but a woman can't, even when she tries, remember the pain of childbirth. She can remember the day, the hour and exactly what she was doing when her labor pains began, but she can't recall the pain. The joy of having a healthy baby far outweighs the discomfort and agony of childbirth. I can't give you a reason, it's just the way it is."

Obviously satisfied with my answer, Jennifer asked, "How long did you stay here?"

"Well, I was here three weeks before you were born, but then..."

Before I could finish my sentence, Jennifer asked another question.

"Was it a nice place?"

"Yes, very nice."

"Were you treated well?"

"Yes, all the girls who came here were treated well. And they were all from very good homes."

"Did you make friends with any of them?"

"No, not really. It was against the rules. But there was a nurse named Gladys whose face resembled an angel. She was a wonderful woman. She was in the labor room and delivery room with me when you were born. A special bond developed between us. I loved Gladys. I feel as if she is with us today."

Tyler, who had been watching me, instinctively realized I was going through a difficult time. Without an explanation or an apology, he turned the key in the ignition and drove away.

My heart pounded. I wanted to let go of the past, and the farther we drove from the maternity home, the better I felt. The next thing I knew, Tyler had pulled in front of the house where I had lived with my family.

When I looked at the beautiful, stately old house, I expected I'd cry, but I didn't feel sad. I felt a sudden burst of emotion – a feeling of strong remorse that I had not been mature enough to recognize the love my family had for me. I thought about the times I doubted my mother's judgment and regretted the times I had momentarily hated her. Realizing my mother had been a truly remarkable woman, I felt a tear escape from my eye. Stubbornly, I brushed it away. I knew that most of my childhood memories were good ones.

Tyler, breaking into my thoughts, asked me if I wanted him to go to the door and ask if the people who live there now would mind if we went through the house.

"No," I said, "I want to remember it just the way it was."

Moments later, as we drove away, I couldn't help but think about Mike.

The rest of the morning was spent showing Jennifer and Ben where I had attended high school: a beautiful school with large buildings and a well-kept campus. We showed them many other places we thought would be interesting to any out-of-town visitor. Jennifer and Ben appeared to be having a wonderful time.

Tyler, who confessed he was hungry and suspected everyone else was hungry, too, suggested we stop for lunch at a popular neighborhood restaurant. He knew it had been my favorite place to eat while I was growing up. I often said they had the best hamburgers in town. As far as I was concerned, they still had the best hamburgers in town. It was unanimously decided that we should eat there.

The restaurant was crowded, so we had to wait for a booth. We were finally seated, and enjoyed our lunch; everyone admitted that the hamburgers were, indeed, well worth waiting for. We talked and laughed as Jennifer and I shared a giant-size chocolate ice cream soda.

After lunch we drove to a park located near my family home. I thought perhaps Tyler chose this particular park because he knew it had a lovely rose garden. And knowing him as well as I did, I suspected he thought I would enjoy spending some quality time alone with my birth daughter.

When we reached the park, Jennifer and I strolled down the path through the rose garden. It was the same path I had walked down so many times when I was a young girl, dreaming romantic dreams of marrying Mike. I remembered when Mike and I had come here to plan our future. Looking into Jennifer's face, I saw Mike. The image of him was there - then it was gone.

It was that precise moment that Jennifer asked me if I would mind telling her something about her birthfather.

"I was just thinking about him," I admitted. I told her about Mike's family, his education, that he had been good in sports and had been a talented artist. In conclusion, I said, "I want you to know that when I was going with your birthfather, although I was very young and foolish, I loved him with all my heart. I want you to know you were conceived in love."

Jennifer responded with a smile, and we held hands as we continued to walk slowly down the path, lined on both sides with beautiful roses of every color, size and description. A few minutes later, she stopped walking, gazed at me and asked, "What should I call you?"

I didn't answer at first because the question took me by surprise. My heart pounded. I was tempted to say, "Please call me Mother." Oh, how I longed to hear the word "Mother" coming from Jennifer's lips, if only one time. But I knew I couldn't say that; she had a mother that she loved. Stalling for time, I nervously twisted my hair and looked at Jennifer, who was patiently waiting for my answer. Then I said, "You can call me Sarah."

"Thank you. I feel comfortable calling you by your first name."

That evening, Jennifer and Ben treated Tyler and me to a delicious steak dinner. Although I was emotionally exhausted, I wouldn't admit it. I wanted to spend as much time as possible with my birth daughter. I still couldn't believe I had found her.

Hours later when the goodbyes were said, it was agreed the four of us would attend church services together the next day.

24

Goodbye....Again

Upon awakening the next morning, I knew it was the last full day I would have to spend with Jennifer. A sinking feeling tugged at my heart. Just thinking about saying goodbye to her made me shudder. I told myself I would have to rely on my inner strength if I wanted to get through this day. Shrugging, I put on a robe and went downstairs. I found Tyler sitting at the kitchen table, reading the Sunday paper and drinking a cup of coffee.

"Good morning, darling," he said as he kissed me. Then he asked how I felt.

"I feel awful. It's like losing her twice."

"I don't understand what you're talking about," said Tyler.

"Well, when Jennifer was a baby, I lost her when I placed her for adoption, and now after all these years, I've found her, only to lose her again, and I..."

Tyler placed his hand over my mouth as he spoke. His words were gentle and kind: "You should concentrate on having a good time with Jennifer. And who knows? It could be the beginning of a wonderful, warm friendship between the two of you."

Two hours later, Tyler and I, accompanied by Jennifer and Ben, were seated in the fourth pew of the beautiful little church I had attended years ago with my parents. The church looked the same except for appearing smaller than I had remembered. Tyler and I had not attended services here since my parents' death. The memories were just too painful for me. I wondered what had prompted me to suggest we come here today. Perhaps it was because I felt a special closeness to God in this church. Maybe it was because I felt close to my parents here. Whatever the reasons, and I wasn't sure what they were, I was nervous.

Thinking about the past, I remembered the happy years I had spent singing in the youth choir. Those were good times to remember. But I frowned when I thought about the day I had married Becca's father Tony right here in this church.

Deliberately pushing memories from the past out of my mind, I concentrated on the sermon. When the minister finished speaking, the congregation recited the Lord's Prayer, the last hymn was sung, and following the benediction, the service was over.

People gathered around us to say hello. I was delighted when many folks remembered my parents and spoke lovingly about them. An elderly woman who had known my parents well gazed at me. Then she gazed at Jennifer - then at me again.

"This beautiful young woman must be your daughter," she said kindly.

As if I had no control over my own words, I responded, "I'd like you to meet my daughter Jennifer."

The instant the words were out of my mouth, I regretted them. I knew I had no right to refer to Jennifer as my daughter. I had given up that right years ago when I had signed the Consent to Adoption paper. I panicked. Closing my eyes, I prayed silently, "Please, God, let Jennifer know that, without thinking, I borrowed her for a moment."

When we left the church, I welcomed the warmth of the sun on my face. Although I tried to control my emotions, tears cascaded down my cheeks as if the safety valve on my heart were breaking from the pressure that had been laid upon it. A painful stab of embarrassment came over me. Then I felt someone gently take my hand.

"Don't worry," Jennifer said, "I understand."

Tyler asked me then if the cafeteria in the Plaza-Center Mall would be a good place to eat dinner.

Grateful to have something as impersonal as Sunday dinner to think about, I composed myself and told him the cafeteria would be just fine. Ben and Jennifer nodded their approval.

Before getting back into the car, Tyler took Polaroid snapshots of Jennifer and me standing on the steps of the picturesque old church. Pictures I knew I would cherish forever.

We drove to the Plaza-Center Mall. The cafeteria was crowded and we had to wait in line almost thirty-five minutes. We were seated finally, and as I listened to the hum of conversation coming from the other tables, I pushed the episode at the church out of my mind. It wasn't long until I was talking, laughing and enjoying myself. I was sure anyone who happened to glance our way would think we were a typical, happy family, out together enjoying a leisurely Sunday dinner.

When we finished eating, Tyler pushed his chair away from the table and confessed he had eaten too much.

"I feel lazy," he said as he attempted unsuccessfully to conceal a yawn. "Would you like to go back to our house so Ben and I can relax and watch television? Perhaps you girls would enjoy visiting or..."

Without giving Tyler a chance to finish, Jennifer interrupted. "I'd like that a lot," she said enthusiastically. "Ben and I don't have much time left. If we want to catch our plane, we have to get up early tomorrow morning and leave the motel no later than seven o'clock."

When Jennifer mentioned leaving, I cringed. Although I was tempted to say, "Please don't go," I said nothing.

When we got home, Tyler and Ben quickly disappeared into the family room where they turned on the television set and watched a special sports event.

Jennifer and I went into the living room and sat down. I asked her if she would like to see a few photographs of my family and me - pictures my parents had taken while I was growing up. When she answered yes, I hurried upstairs to get them.

Jennifer scooted closer to me as we looked at the pictures.

"Your parents were distinguished-looking people," she commented. "And I know you must miss them a lot, but have you ever thought about looking for your birth mother?"

"Yes, I'm in the process of searching for her now. However, it won't be easy to find her. All the records from the maternity home where I was born were destroyed by fire several years ago."

"Oh, I hope and pray that you find her. Then the two of us will know what nationality we are. And I'd love to know something about her; after all, she's my birth grandmother."

"Well, I'm not one to give up easily," I said, watching Jennifer thumb through the old family albums.

I was pleased with my birth daughter. It was obvious she had had social, educational and financial advantages given her. I believed she possessed a gentle wholesomeness, yet a certain unmistakable flair of sophistication, too. Jennifer was poised, polite and gracious with a quiet pleasing personality. Anyone would be proud to call her their daughter.

The remainder of the afternoon literally flew by while Jennifer and I enjoyed visiting. Jennifer told me little personal things about herself, including the fact that she had a temper.

"Well, don't worry about it," I said. "I'm sure you'll outgrow it - I did."

We laughed.

I felt good inside.

I wanted to reach out and hug Jennifer, but I was afraid she'd break. I wanted to tell her how much I loved her, but I was afraid I'd frighten her away.

When Jennifer and Ben walked out the front door that night to return to their motel, my heart sank.

When I awakened early the next morning, I felt sick inside. I was afraid that when I told Jennifer goodbye I'd burst into tears. Although I couldn't bear the thought of her leaving, I told myself I had to be strong for Jennifer's sake.

Holding that thought in mind, I arrived with Tyler at the motel thirty-five minutes later. We waited at a deserted pool-side table for Jennifer and Ben to come down from their room.

When they appeared, Ben hurriedly explained they had overslept and were running late. He politely shook hands with me, bent, kissed my cheek and smiled warmly.

"I'm glad I met you," he said. "And thanks for showing us such a good time."

With Tyler's help, Ben took their luggage to their rented car and loaded it into the trunk.

My birth daughter and I were left alone. We gazed into each other's faces. We embraced. Softly, yet clearly, Jennifer said, "I would have been proud to have called you Mother all my life."

Then she turned and walked away. Not once did she look back.

25

Let's Make a Deal

For a long time after Jennifer left to return to her familiar surroundings – the only life she had ever known – I lay around the house and cried. I relived every moment I had shared with her. I was emotionally drained. It was, indeed, like losing her twice. Although she had no way of knowing, Jennifer had taken a large part of my heart with her. I had the same empty feeling I had had the day I left the maternity home without her, and the feeling hurt. Yet I thanked God for having found her alive and well. I thanked God for what I considered a miracle.

Six weeks later when I returned to the monthly meeting of the search and support group, I was feeling a little better and shared the experience of our reunion with the others. Everyone was pleased that I had found my birth daughter. Then someone asked if I were still planning to search for my birth mother.

"Absolutely!" I said. When I started the search, it was my goal to find the two of them, and that's exactly what I intend to do."

All the members of the group stood up and applauded. They assured me I could count on them for their continued support. When the meeting was over, I asked Joan if she would assist me in my second search.

With a long, drawn-out sigh, Joan said, "Well, what you went through to find your birth daughter will seem easy compared to the struggle you'll probably be facing when you try to locate your birth mother. But I'll help you as much as I can. Do you have much information about her?"

"Very little. However, I have a copy of the Consent to Adoption paper she signed. From this I learned her name was Marie and that she named me Marilyn. Shortly after my parents died," I explained, "I found a hand-written letter that the administrator of the home where I had been born had sent to my adoptive parents. The letter described Marie as an attractive twenty-two year old college student who..."

"Sarah, before you say another word, I must tell you there's an inside joke among the members of the search and support group that every birth mother was an attractive twenty-two year old college student who was five foot five inches tall, weighed approximately 110 pounds, possessed a wonderful sweet disposition and was musically gifted. Fifty percent of them were described as cheerleaders who intended to return to college after the birth of their babies. Such descriptive letters often contained false information."

"But why?"

"Well," said Joan with a shrug, "if the birth mother happened to be a young girl who was only thirteen or fourteen years old, the administrator of the home lied about her age. You see, most couples wanted to adopt a baby whose biological mother was in her late teens or early twenties - a college student who was on the honor roll and musically gifted - someone who resembled Miss America. There are approximately five million adoptees in the United States, and you know very well that all their birth mothers couldn't have fit such descriptions."

"Then you're telling me that the administrators wrote letters with descriptions of the birth mothers that looked good on paper?"

"Exactly."

"You mean the letter I found that was written about my birth mother wasn't true?"

"It could have been true, but it probably wasn't."

Now I was discouraged before I had even started searching for the only woman in the world who could answer my questions concerning my background. Perhaps it was a waste of time to try to locate her, I told myself. Then Joan said there was a possibility my birth mother had stayed in this area after my birth. She suggested I look through the marriage records and informed me they were indexed, open to the public and easy to use.

The next morning, Tyler and I went to the Hall of Records and, with the help of an obliging clerk, checked the marriage records starting with the year of my birth and for the next ten years. But we were unable to find my birth mother's name listed as a bride anywhere. We assumed she had returned to wherever she had come from - anywhere in the United States. I was again discouraged.

In the meantime, I received friendly letters from Jennifer, a lovely birthday gift, and even a Mother's Day gift! I believed our relationship was progressing well.

Tyler took early retirement, thus having more time available to help me search. Although there were times when I was discouraged, I was too stubborn to give up the search.

Then one day I had an idea. It was a long shot, I thought, yet well worth pursuing. I made up my mind that somehow I would obtain my original birth certificate, even though I knew the original certificate was sealed and couldn't be opened without a court order. I had always known adoptees had two birth certificates. One was called the original, bearing the name of the birth mother, her occupation, what she had named her baby and usually the name of the state she had come from along with the name of the attending physician. The other birth certificate was amended and sometimes was referred to as the altered birth certificate that showed the names of the adoptive parents along with the name they had chosen for the baby. Knowing this, I felt certain that if I could somehow manage to get my original birth certificate, the task of locating my birth mother would be a lot easier.

So, before I could change my mind, I picked up the telephone and dialed the number for the Division of Vital Statistics. "What do I have to lose?" I asked myself aloud. Impatiently, I waited for someone to answer.

"Hello, may I help you?" asked a clerk.

"Yes, I need your help, and I'm willing to pay for it."

There was silence for a moment. I wondered if the clerk had hung up.

"Are you there?" I inquired.

"Yes," came a hesitant reply.

"Please don't hang up until you've given me an opportunity to explain," I said with a definite tone of urgency. I told the clerk I was terminally ill and had only a short time to live. "I'm adopted and desperately need to locate my biological mother. All I want from you is a copy of my original birth certificate."

"I can't help you. I can't break the rules. If I did, I'd lose my job, and I..."

"You wouldn't lose your job," I argued, "you would make a lot of extra money. Now don't tell me you couldn't use it."

"Of course I could use the money - who couldn't? My husband's out of work and we're expecting our first baby. That's why I can't risk losing my job; if I did I would lose my health insurance."

"My dear, " I said, almost yelling, "you won't lose anything. No one will ever know."

"Maybe I should think it over," the clerk said, obviously beginning to weaken.

"I'll pay you cash!"

"Well, I'm not promising you I'll help you, but if you want, you can call me back in thirty minutes."

Twenty-five minutes later, I nervously dialed the phone, and when the clerk answered - I recognized her voice - I said, "Oh, I just know you've decided to help me."

"No, not I. It was my husband who decided we needed the extra money."

That afternoon, Tyler and I met the clerk's husband at the Midtown Shopping Mall. Before I handed the envelope containing $500 to the fidgety-looking young man, I told him I wanted to check the file number on the original birth certificate to see if it matched the number on the amended certificate. When I saw the file numbers were the same, I handed him the envelope, took the original birth certificate, thanked him and made a hasty departure.

Hurrying to the car, I gazed at the document I had just purchased. On the right hand side on line sixteen, I saw under "Mother's birthplace" the name of the state she had come from. When I looked on line seventeen, I saw listed under "Mother's occupation" the words "college student." On line seventeen A, following "Mother's age at last birthday", I saw that my birth mother had been twenty-two years old at the time of my birth, just as the descriptive letter had stated.

"Tyler," I said. "It looks as though the information in the letter describing my birth mother was correct."

26

Up in Smoke

T he next day I told Joan I had a copy of my original birth certificate in my possession, and knew what state my birth mother
had come from. Although she asked how I had obtained it, I refused to tell her. Deliberately, I did not pursue the subject; instead I asked her what I should do next.

"Well," Joan said, realizing I wasn't going to reveal my source, "you
should go to the National Archives and look through the 1910 census.
From that you can learn the name of the county your birth mother
came from, thus narrowing down your search."

Monday morning, Tyler and I were waiting outside the door when
the National Archives opened. The volunteers helped us use the soundex coding guide so that we could find the correct microfilm to look
through. A volunteer told me that the 1910 census had been hand-
written on index cards and years later transferred onto the microfilm.

When I stared at the monitor and studied the list of names, I was
upset to see that most of them were illegible. It wasn't long until I had a
throbbing headache. I saw spots in front of my eyes, but I kept going
and looked through a lot of names. When the archives closed their
doors that evening, I was no closer to locating my birth mother than I
had been before. Disillusioned, I wondered if I would ever find her. On
the way home, I twisted my hair and stared out the car window.

"Sarah, you're so quiet," said Tyler. "Quit twisting your hair and tell
me what you're thinking about."

"I was thinking that perhaps I should forget about trying to locate
my birth mother and go on with the rest of my life. Maybe I should be
grateful I found Jennifer and let it go at that."

"You're giving up prematurely," Tyler said. "Remember, there are
people who have been searching for years. I know you're discouraged
now, but after you get a good night's sleep, you'll feel different."

As Tyler had predicted, the next morning when I awoke, I felt better and tenaciously continued the search. I wrote query letters to the Motor Vehicle Department, the Voter Registration Office and the Social Security Administration in an attempt to locate my birth mother. Then I had another idea.

Hurrying to the library, I copied the names of the colleges and universities that had been in operation during the years my birth mother had been in attendance. When I returned home, I wrote a query letter to the registrars of forty-nine colleges and universities that were located in the state she had come from. The letter read:

> *To the Registrar:*
>
> *Due to a separation in my family, I lost contact with my aunt whose name is Marie Nelson. She was enrolled in your school during the years 1927, 1928, and 1929.*
>
> *It is very important that I locate her, for she has recently inherited a large sum of money. If you find her name listed in your records, please notify me as soon as possible.*
>
> *Cordially,*
> *Sarah Smith*

After the query letters were addressed and stamped, I hurried to the post office and mailed them. I told myself I had done all I could do; there was nothing left to do but wait.

Waiting had never been one of my virtues. I had been told often that I was a good cook, a good mother to Becca and a loving wife to Tyler, but I had never been told I was a patient person. In fact, I was sure that my inability to practice patience infuriated Tyler.

I was right. That evening when we finished eating dinner, he turned to me and said, "I think the search is affecting your health." He suggested I concentrate on other things: "Have lunch with a friend. Read a good book. Don't let the search become an obsession. And above all, don't be so impatient," he warned.

Taking my husband's advice, I read several books. I had lunch with a few friends, but all I could think about was finding my birth mother. I had wanted to find her for as many years as I could remember. I was tired of looking into the mirror and wondering if there was someone in the world who looked like me. At night, I had trouble falling asleep. I kept shifting positions, and when I did sleep, I dreamed about meeting my birth mother face to face. Then I would wake up with a start, nervous perspiration dripping from my forehead, when I realized it was just a dream.

Then one day, the replies from the registrars started arriving. Enthusiastically, I opened one letter after another. All the replies were kind, considerate and showed genuine interest in my search for my aunt. Unfortunately, all of them read something like this:

Dear Ms. Sarah Smith:

Please be advised that I looked through our records and could find no evidence that your aunt attended this institution. I am sorry that I couldn't help you, but I wish you luck in your endeavor.

Sincerely,
Rose Rogers, Registrar

The replies that followed were similar. It wasn't long before I was very depressed. I reminded myself that I had not received all the replies. Determined to find the woman to whom I was truly related, I kept hoping; then the replies stopped coming.

Weeks went by. Reluctantly I thought about giving up the search. My emotions continued to plummet. The days seemed endless, but the nights were the worst. During the daytime hours, I told myself I had given up, but late at night when I got into bed, I asked God to help me find my birthmother. Down deep inside, I hadn't given up. I couldn't give up, nor could I ignore the possibility that somewhere out there, someone was perhaps waiting for me.

Then it happened: I went to the mailbox and found a letter that had been accidentally sent to the wrong address. Hurriedly, I tore open the envelope and read aloud:

Dear Ms. Sarah Smith:

I am in receipt of your letter regarding the whereabouts of your aunt.

According to our records, we had a student by the name Jessica Marie Nelson in attendance during the years you inquired about. However, she transferred to another university.

If you wish further information about your aunt, you should get in touch with their Alumni Association.

Sincerely yours,
Mary Mead, Registrar

Without hesitating for even a minute, I picked up the telephone and dialed information for the number of the Alumni Association. When I was given the number, I placed a call and waited for someone to answer. When a woman answered, I identified myself and asked her if she would look through her records for a former student by the name Jessica Marie Nelson.

"Yes, I'll be glad to look through our records," she answered. "But it will take me about an hour, because all those records are in the basement."

"Thank you," I said. "I'll call you back in an hour."

Less than an hour later, I excitedly dialed the phone and when the woman answered, I asked, "Did you find my aunt? Do you have her address?"

"Yes, I found her," said the woman. "Do you have a pencil?"

117

"Do I have a ... what?"

"Do you have a pencil?" she asked again.

Losing my patience, I screamed into the mouthpiece, "Yes, I have a pencil. Please give me her address."

"I'm sorry, I don't have her address. All I have is the name of the town she came from."

My hand shook as I carefully wrote down the name of a town on a piece of paper. I thanked the woman.

"I'm glad I could help you," she said. "You shouldn't have any trouble locating your aunt; the town she came from is small. If you call the high school - there's only one - and talk to the principal, I'm sure he'll be able to help you."

Thanking the woman again, I replaced the receiver and redialed the phone. This time I called information in the town my birth mother had come from. When the operator gave me the number for the high school, I immediately dialed it. When someone answered, I asked to speak to the principal. Moments later, a man said, "Hello, may I help you?"

I told him who I was and whom I was looking for. I asked him if he would please check his records. When he returned to the phone, he said, "I'm sorry, but there's no record of a former student by that name. You must have been given the wrong information."

"You must be mistaken!"

"No, I looked through my records twice."

Hanging up the phone, I shivered. The excitement I had felt a few minutes before had been replaced by a chill of disappointment. I was about to cry when I smelled something burning.

"Oh, Lord, the meat loaf!"

I had forgotten to take our dinner out of the oven. I ran into the kitchen. A cloud of thick smoke billowed from the stove. The odor of burned meat permeated the air. Turning off the oven, I grabbed hot pads and removed the meat loaf. It was burned beyond recognition. It looked like a piece of charred leather. I pulled out a chair, held my head in both hands and sobbed. I was still sitting there crying when Tyler came home.

"Sarah, what happened?" he asked.

"Oh, I thought I had found my birth mother, but it turned out to be only a false lead...and I burned the meat loaf. Dinner is ruined."

"If you're not careful," he said, "you're going to ruin more than a meal. You're going to ruin your life. Sarah, you can't go on like this. You spend every minute searching for your birth mother. And you're still worn out from the search and reunion with Jennifer. Now it looks as though you can't find your birth mother. Maybe the two of us should take a little vacation. Would you like that?"

"No, I'd feel just as bad somewhere else as I do right here," I said as I dumped the burned meat loaf down the garbage disposal.

While Tyler waited in the car, I ran upstairs to change clothes to go out to dinner. The phone rang. It rang several times, but I didn't answer it. "I don't feel like talking to anyone," I mumbled.

27

Let This Be It

Long after Tyler drifted into a sound sleep that night and was snoring softly, I was wide awake with troubled thoughts. Searching had been a strain on my nerves and emotions, but I hated to surrender to defeat. Finding my birth mother had been a life-long dream. If crying would have helped any, I would have cried uncontrollably. Finally, I slept.

Upon awakening the next morning, I slowly got out of bed, stretched and walked into the bathroom where I found a note taped to the mirror:

Sarah, dear,

When I got up this morning, I decided to take my boat and go fishing with Jerry. I'll be home around five thirty.

Love, Tyler

I shrugged. I told myself although Tyler liked to go fishing with his friend Jerry, I suspected he wanted a good excuse to get out of the house and away from me – not that I blamed him. No one knew better than I did that I had been very difficult to live with lately.

Getting dressed, I went downstairs and sat down at the kitchen table to have a cup of coffee and read the morning paper. I was pouring myself a second cup of coffee when the telephone rang. I thought perhaps it was Becca calling, so I answered the phone.

"Hello," came a voice on the other end of the line. "I've been trying to reach you ever since yesterday evening."

Not recognizing the voice, I asked, "Who is this please?"

"Oh, I'm terribly sorry, I should have identified myself. I'm Mrs. Miller, the woman you spoke with from the Alumni Association concerning your aunt. I'm afraid I made a dreadful mistake."

119

"A mistake?"

"Yes. And I feel bad about it. When you called me back yesterday, I gave you the wrong information. The paper our old records are written on is old and fragile. When I turned the page, I accidentally turned two pages. I gave you the name of the wrong town for your aunt."

The anxiety I had suffered during the search for my birth mother was nothing compared to the anxiety I was experiencing now. I twisted and untwisted the telephone cord. Excitement surged within me. But I wondered if I had heard her correctly.

"Are you sure you have the right town now?" I asked.

"Yes, I'm quite certain."

The remainder of the conversation was brief. Mrs. Miller gave me the name of the correct town for my birth mother.

"I'm sure," said Mrs. Miller, "that you'll be able to find her. She then said goodbye and hung up.

"She didn't give me an opportunity to thank her," I murmured as I placed a long-distance call to the high school in the town where my birth mother had grown up. Nervously, I paced the floor. I heard the phone ring three times. Then a woman answered, "Hello, may I help you?"

"Yes, I'd like to speak to the principal."

Again I had to wait.

A few seconds later, a man said, "This is Mr. Johnston. How may I help you?"

At once I told him I was searching for my aunt who had recently inherited a large sum of money. I stared at the floor, ashamed of myself for repeating the fabrication concerning my "aunt". But my theory was a simple one: I believed people would be more willing to help me search for my birth mother if they thought she was my aunt, and if a large amount of money were involved. I had learned from some of the search and support group members that sometimes unorthodox methods were used when a person was trying to find someone. But I had also been told that it was important not to create embarrassing situations for anyone. I believed the story about my aunt's inheritance would cause no harm to anyone. So I gave Mr. Johnston my birth mother's maiden name and the approximate time she would have been in attendance at his school. I asked him if he would please look through his old records.

"Yes, I'll be glad to look through them," he replied. "I'll put you on hold."

Involuntarily listening to elevator music, I closed my eyes and prayed, "Please, God, let this be it."

Finally the music stopped. I heard Mr. Johnston's voice.

"According to our records," he said, "your aunt was graduated from this high school June 5, 1927."

Joy filled my heart. I felt like letting myself go - like shouting! But I didn't. Instead I said, "Do you know if my aunt still lives around there?"

"I'm terribly sorry, but I don't know," he answered. "I've lived here only a year, but I know a local woman who might remember your aunt. You should get in touch with Miss Callie Ann. This is a small town, and Miss Callie Ann, a seventy-eight year old woman, has lived here all her life. If anyone can help you, she can."

"How do I get in touch with her?"

"I'll give you her phone number........I have it here somewhere...."

A few seconds later, I dialed the phone and asked to speak to Miss Callie Ann.

"This is she," a woman answered.

"You don't know me," I began, "but I'm searching for my aunt. Her name is Jessica Marie Nelson, and I was told you might know her."

"You say you're her niece?"

"Yes."

A silence followed.

Stirring my coffee, I took a sip, swallowed and nervously waited for Miss Callie Ann to say something.

"May I ask you a question?"

"Yes, of course."

"Tell me, dear, how old are you?"

Taken by surprise and not wanting to reveal my age to a total stranger, I said, "Well, I'm in my early fifties."

"And you say you're looking for your aunt?"

"That's right. It's very important that I find her."

"May I ask you a personal question?"

"Of course."

"Are you by any chance adopted and looking for your real mother?"

Speechless, I pulled out a chair and sat down. I wondered how she knew, but before I could ask, she voluntarily told me.

"My dear, your mother and I have been friends for many years. I know she doesn't have a niece, but when she was a young girl, she had a baby out of wedlock. Today that baby would be in her early fifties."

"Oh......?"

"Are you Jessica's daughter?" Miss Callie Ann asked.

"Yes, I am."

"Why did you tell me you were looking for your aunt?"

"Because I wanted to protect my birth mother."

Evidently satisfied with my answer, Miss Callie Ann told me she had always had a strong feeling that someday Jessica's daughter would come looking for her.

"I've thought about searching for my birth mother ever since I was a little girl," I told her. "And now, more than anything else, I want to meet her. Do you know where she lives? Did she ever marry? And if so, do you know her married name?"

"One question at a time, my dear."

"I'm sorry, but I've never come this close to finding her before. She is still alive...?"

"Yes, she is alive and doing well."

"How can I get in touch with her?"

121

"I'm not sure I should be the one to tell you. But I can tell you something about her."

I wanted to scream at this woman, "Please tell me how I can locate my birth mother!" But I didn't want to be rude to an elderly woman who could possibly help me find Jessica, so I listened politely as Miss Callie Ann explained that she and Jessica had been good friends since childhood.

"We went through grade school, high school and started college together," she said. "In those days, your mother was a fun-loving cheerful young woman. She and I had many good times, and we went everywhere together. Then all of a sudden, when we were in our second year of college, Jessica announced she was leaving school. Although she didn't give me a reason, I knew she was pregnant."

"How did you know?"

"Well, we came from a small town. Everyone knew everything about everyone. You know how some folks love to gossip."

"Yes, unfortunately, I do, and I..."

Before I could go on, Miss Callie Ann interrupted and told me Jessica didn't know she knew. "She doesn't know to this day, and that's the reason I'm not sure I should tell you how to get in touch with her, yet..."

"I'll never tell her," I promised. "It will be our little secret."

"Well, it would probably do Jessica a world of good to know the baby she placed for adoption so many years ago is all right. I imagine she's wondered about you."

"I'm sure she has, and I would appreciate it very much if you would help me find her, for her sake as well as mine."

"I need time to think," Miss Callie Ann said. Then, as if she were enjoying every minute of it, she rattled on and on about my birth mother.

"After you were born, your mother transferred to another university. When she was graduated, she never came back here to live. She and her family moved to a town about seventy-five miles west of here. Jessica and I were no longer close, but we still kept in touch. Ten years later - or maybe it was eleven years later - no, it was ten, Jessica married. Two years after that, she and her husband had a baby girl."

"I have a half-sister?"

"Yes, but I know she doesn't know anything about you. I'm certain that Jessica never told a living soul she had had a baby out of wedlock. In those days, it was considered a sin - a terrible scandal."

Nodding, I listened to Miss Callie Ann and wondered if she would ever get around to telling me what I wanted to know. When she didn't, I lost my patience and blurted out, "Please! Just tell me how to get in touch with my birth mother!" A moment later, I regretted the outburst and explained that I had been searching for a long time.

Miss Callie Ann must have heard the urgency and sheer determination in my voice, for without further hesitation she gave me Jessica's married name and her address.

28

Scared to Death

N ow everything was going too fast for me. I picked up the telephone. I dialed information for my birth mother's number. Once I had it, I redialed, but quickly replaced the receiver. I knew I had to deal with the dilemma of whether to telephone her or visit her in person.

Undecided, I said aloud, "There's always the possibility she could hang up the telephone on me. But if I go see her and appear on her doorstep, she could slam the door in my face." Confused, I glanced at the clock and saw it was almost five-thirty. Tyler would be home soon.

Stretching out on the couch, I fought the urge to call my birth mother, but I wanted to talk it over with Tyler before I did anything I might regret later. I closed my eyes and thought about Jessica and wondered what I would say, and how I would say it, when I introduced myself to her. The next thing I remember, I saw Tyler staring down at me. Smiling, he sat in a nearby chair.

"Sarah," he said, "you slept here all night."

"Why didn't you wake me?"

"Because I thought you needed your rest. Maybe you don't realize it, but you're emotionally exhausted, and you looked so peaceful sleeping there...."

"Oh, Tyler," I said, interrupting, "I have something unbelievable to tell you. Yesterday while you were gone....."

When I finished telling Tyler about finding my birth mother, I paused to catch my breath. Then I asked him if I should telephone her or go see her.

"Sarah, that must be your decision."

Without another word, I reached for the telephone. I had decided I couldn't wait another minute before talking to my birth mother.

"Wait..!" Tyler said. "Give yourself a little time to think about it. Come into the kitchen with me and have a cup of coffee, and it might be a good idea if you call Joan and ask for her advice. After all, she's had years of experience with this sort of thing."

As I poured myself a cup of coffee, I telephoned Joan. We talked for quite awhile. When I hung up, I excitedly told Tyler it was Joan's suggestion that we get into our car and go visit my birth mother.

He looked surprised and asked how Joan had come to that conclusion.

"Well, when I told Joan I had learned from Miss Callie Ann that Jessica is a widow with a grown daughter, we assumed she must live alone. Joan pointed out that if I telephoned her, it would be too easy for her to hang up the phone, but if I went to see her, she..."

"Oh, Sarah, wouldn't that be a terrible shock?"

"Yes, but it will be traumatic for her no matter what method of self-introduction I choose. If I go see her, stand on her doorstep and ring the doorbell, at least when she answers the door I'll be able to see what she looks like. And Joan told me Jessica will probably be as curious about me as I am about her. So I'd like to leave today."

Exuberantly, I bounded up the stairs and packed two suitcases. Less than thirty minutes later, I returned to the kitchen where I found Tyler busily studying a map.

"It will take us about two and a half days to get there," he said. "Are you ready to leave?"

"Yes, but before we go, there's something I have to do. I want to call my brother."

Before Tyler had an opportunity to ask me why I wanted to talk to Frank, I had already dialed the phone. Tears filled my eyes as I told my brother about locating my birth mother. Then pausing a long moment, I asked, "Do you think it would hurt Mother and Dad if I met Jessica?"

"Mother and Dad are dead, " Frank said. "You can't hurt them. But, Sarah, you could get hurt. Have you thought about this - what if your birth mother doesn't want to be found? What if she rejects you? And you should realize," he went on, "there's no guarantee you'll like whom you find. You don't know anything about her. Yet on the other hand," Frank said thoughtfully, "I know you've been curious about her ever since you were a child. It's just that I'd hate to see you get hurt. But don't worry, you can't hurt Mother and Dad."

"Frank, what about you?" I asked. "Would you be hurt or upset if I went to see my birth mother?"

"No, Sarah, I understand."

"Then I have your blessing?"

"Well, you have my approval."

Tyler and I had driven only a short time when he glanced over at me and asked, "Why are you twisting your hair? What's bothering you?"

"I'm worried about the outcome of this trip."

"Are you concerned about possible rejection?"

"I'm scared to death! I've heard conflicting stories from members of the support group. There have been cases where the birth mother was overjoyed to meet her birth son or daughter. But there have been many cases where the birth mother refused to acknowledge the baby she placed for adoption. I don't know what to expect from Jessica. I'm not sure I can deal with rejection."

"Don't anticipate trouble," Tyler said.

"But, Tyler, you don't realize what I'm going through. I've always yearned to belong, to find my birth mother, and yet I repeated the process in my own life: a heart-rending experience. Now my search for self is about to end - how it will end is what worries me."

"Sarah, you worry too much. Try to think good thoughts. Relax and enjoy the beautiful scenery, and please, dear, quit twisting your hair."

That evening when we stopped at a motel, I was glad the first day of driving was over. After we showered, we found a nice restaurant for dinner. Later at the motel, although I was tired, it was hours before I fell asleep.

The next morning after a light breakfast, we started on our journey again. I felt as if I were going somewhere I had been before. It was a weird feeling that I couldn't explain even to myself, so I didn't try to explain it to Tyler. Then I thought about the events that had brought me to this point in my life. I knew I had not given myself a chance to come to terms with what a difference a day made. Less than twenty-four hours before, I had assumed I would never find my birth mother. Now I was on my way to meet her. My dream of finding my roots was about to come true. I was frightened. If I acted irrational, who could blame me?

After an uneventful eight and a half hours of driving, we found a motel, had a bite to eat, and because I was emotionally exhausted and tired of driving, I welcomed sleep.

The next morning we dressed, ate breakfast and were back in the car before seven o'clock. The sun should have been coming up, but it wasn't. Large raindrops freckled the windshield, followed by a torrential downpour, rendering the windshield wipers useless. We couldn't see to drive, nor could we see to stop driving. It was dark as night, and I sat quietly and shook inside.

"Don't worry," said Tyler reassuringly. "We're driving through an early morning cloudburst. You'll see - the rain will stop as abruptly as it began."

Less than twenty minutes later, as Tyler had predicted, the rain let up. There was, however, a dense fog hanging heavily over the open fields. Visibility, I guessed, was less than a city block. I had to squint my eyes to see the highway. Then the sun broke through the dark clouds and burned off the fog. The world looked bright and clean. When I opened the car window, the sweet smell of freshly cut alfalfa reached my nostrils. I saw a spectacular multi-colored rainbow arched in the sky and remembered that my grandmother had told me often a rainbow was a special sign from God, promising better times.

29

For A Lifetime

At two o'clock that afternoon, we drove into a small town where my birth mother had made her home for many years. I was nervous and clutched Jessica's address tightly in my closed hand. We drove around the picturesque town square - a town square that looked as if it came out of an old western movie. Then Tyler saw the police station and parked the car.

"Wait here a minute," he said. "I'm going inside and ask for directions."

As I waited, I tapped my foot and lit one cigarette after another. What's keeping him? I asked myself. When Tyler returned finally, he was smiling.

"The police chief is going to escort us to your birth mother's house," Tyler announced proudly.

"Oh, that's great. All we need - a police escort..."

"He's not going to drive his squad car into her living room. He's only trying to be polite to an out-of-town visitor." Tyler started the car, made a U-turn and followed the police chief. Minutes later, the squad car slowed down. The police chief pointed to a pretty white house on the left-hand side of the street, waved and drove on.

"Sarah, we're here," Tyler said as he drove into the driveway and stopped the car.

I couldn't move. I sat there and stared at the house. I was so shaken that I could hardly breathe. I felt sick all the way down to my toes - sick from fear. "I don't feel very good," I told Tyler. "I'm not sure I can go through with this, and..."

"Sarah, you're going to get out of the car and walk to the front door with me. There's someone in there you've always wanted to meet."

Before I could argue, Tyler ran around the car and opened the door. He helped me get out. "Don't be frightened, he said, "Remember, I'm right here with you."

Then, with Tyler's help, I put one foot in front of the other and slowly walked toward the house. When we reached the front porch, I stumbled. Carefully, I stepped onto the porch and stood back while Tyler knocked on the door. I shook inside. I hid behind Tyler while I waited for my birth mother to answer the door. My knees buckled. My heart pounded. The door opened.

Overcome with curiosity, I peeked around my husband's shoulder and saw a woman standing in the open doorway. I stared at her wide-eyed. For the first time in my life, I knew there was someone in the world who looked like me.

"Are you Jessica Marie Nelson?" asked Tyler.

"Yes," answered the woman. Then, puzzled, she asked, "Do I know you?"

"No, you don't know us," Tyler responded, "but we've come a long way to meet you, and we..."

"To meet *me?*"

"Yes, and we have something very important to talk to you about."

Not able to stand the suspense for another moment, I stepped out from behind Tyler's back and gazed into my birth mother's face. Stammering, I said, "What I have to say to you is important to me - important to both of us."

"I don't understand," Jessica replied.

"Well, I don't know exactly where to begin." I took a deep breath, stalled for time and whispered, "I guess the only sensible thing to do is just come right out and tell you..."

"Tell me *what?*" Jessica interrupted, obviously irritated.

The annoyance I heard in my birth mother's voice frightened me. I wanted to throw my arms around her and say, "I belong to you. I'm the baby you relinquished for adoption so many, many years ago." But I couldn't say that. I felt awkward and tongue-tied. I reminded myself I had dreamed about this moment for a lifetime. Here I was, standing in front of my birth mother, yet I didn't know what to say. I forgot about the carefully worded speech I had rehearsed, cleared my throat and asked, "Does April 7, 1932, mean anything to you?"

"No."

"It should. That's the day I was born."

"I'm sorry, but it doesn't mean a thing."

Confused, I felt helpless as if I were sinking into quicksand. I had expected my birth mother would be shocked, but I had hoped and prayed she would acknowledge me. I looked at Tyler. I looked back at Jessica and said, "Surely you remember..."

"You've made a mistake. I don't know who you are or what you want."

Realizing I was getting nowhere and tired of playing games, I decided to come right out and tell Jessica who I was.

"My parents adopted me. I'm the baby you placed for adoption."

A long, awkward silence followed. The color drained out of my birth mother's face. A look of astonishment filled her eyes.

"You have the wrong person," she cried out.

"No, I have the right person. You're my birth mother and I have proof."

"My dear girl, you've made a terrible mistake," Jessica reiterated loudly.

As I stood there listening to Jessica, I heard pain and aggravation in her voice. I saw a look of undeniable fear in her pale, drawn face. In my mind's eye, I could imagine exactly what she was going through. It was not long ago I had gone through a similar experience when I met Jennifer. And I knew this unsuspecting, sweet-looking elderly woman couldn't have, even in her wildest dreams, anticipated that the baby she had placed for adoption would suddenly appear on her doorstep. The strong urge to hug her tugged at my heart. Oh, how I wanted to comfort her - to tell her everything would be all right.

Groping for the right words, I pleaded, "Please listen to me. I didn't come here to hurt you. The last thing I want is to frighten you." Reaching into my purse, I pulled out the manila envelope that contained my original birth certificate and the Consent to Adoption paper Jessica had signed.

Tyler, who had been a silent bystander up until now, took a step forward and smiled at Jessica. "You have no idea what my wife has gone through to locate you," he said. "She's come a long way to meet you. She doesn't want to cause you any trouble. She just wants to sit down and talk with you. But I can see," he added, "we're upsetting you, so we'll leave now. But for your sake as well as Sarah's, I suggest you look through the contents of this envelope. When you do, you'll know that my wife is who she says she is." Turning, Tyler took my arm and gently led me off the porch.

Pulling away from him, I stared at my birth mother. Tears rolled steadily down my face. The sting of rejection hurt.

"All my life," I murmured, "I've dreamed about meeting you. For a lifetime I've wondered about you. All I want is an opportunity to sit down and talk with you."

For an instant, Jessica looked as if she were about to say something, but she must have changed her mind, for she didn't say a single word.

Slowly, I walked to the car with Tyler. Just before I got into the car, I looked back at Jessica and said loud enough for her to hear me, "I have confidence that after you've had time to get over the shock and think about it, you'll be as thrilled as I am. And rest assured, I'll be back tomorrow."

30

A Bond
That Goes Beyond

The minute we were back in the car, Tyler turned to me and asked, "How you you feel?"

"I feel all right and I'm not as upset as I thought I would be," I told him. "Under the circumstances I think I handled myself rather well."

"Yes, you certainly did. I'm proud of you."

"Thank you. But I'm disappointed my birth mother didn't throw her arms around me the instant I introduced myself to her, yet I realize denial on her part isn't all that uncommon. I remember reading in the book *SEARCH: A HANDBOOK FOR ADOPTEES AND BIRTHPARENTS*, by Jayne Askin with Bob Oskam, that the initial contact you eventually make will be a surprising, emotional event for the other person. In the same book it said 'Don't be too quick to assume you've been totally rejected.' It's easy for me to comprehend how my birth mother feels. I imagine my sudden appearance on her porch was the most phenomenal shock she's ever lived through."

"I agree with you," said Tyler. "So don't get discouraged. After Jessica has had a chance to put her thoughts into the proper perspective, she'll probably accept you. There's no doubt in your mind that she's your birth mother...is there?"

"Absolutely no doubt at all. Not only do I have proof she's my biological mother, you saw her - she looks like me."

Nodding, Tyler glanced at his watch. "It's past seven o'clock," he said. "Aren't you hungry?"

"Yes, I'm starved!"

"Well, what do you say we find a restaurant, have a hot dinner, register at a nice motel and then get a good night's sleep. I have a feeling you're in for a big day tomorrow."

When the sun rose the next morning, I opened my eyes and thought about the day ahead of me. I promised myself I would exercise understanding and patience where Jessica was concerned. I also promised myself I wouldn't leave town until I had had an opportunity to talk with her. I'd come too far to turn back.

An hour later, Tyler and I got into our car and drove to Jessica's house. This time my determination to visit with my birth mother outweighed my fear. Hurrying to the front door, I knocked and then stood back and waited.

The door opened. I looked over my shoulder to see if Tyler were there to give me moral support. As usual, he was there, smiling down at me.

Jessica unlocked the screen door - the only thing separating us. She reached out and took my hand in hers and said, "Please come in."

I felt as if I were moving in slow motion through someone else's dream. And I knew I would remember this moment forever. There was a lump in my throat and tears in my eyes.

Jessica politely invited us into her living room and asked us to sit down.

I sat in the nearest chair and nervously twisted a handkerchief.

Jessica started to say something, but changed her mind. I saw tears rolling down her face.

Tyler broke the awkward silence, "Thank you for inviting us into your home."

I just sat there and gazed at my birth mother who was, in my opinion, an attractive woman with a flair of elegance. Her hair was dark brown like mine, except hers was streaked with strands of silver gray. Her large hazel eyes were exactly like mine. Our bone structure was similar, too. For a woman her age - seventy nine - I thought she had a youthful look about her. She was smaller than I, and rather thin, but there was a strong family likeness between us. I couldn't explain it, but I had the most peculiar feeling I had seen her before. What I had seen, of course, was my own reflection in the mirror. There was, indeed, someone in the world who looked a lot like me. As I continued to gaze at her, I noticed that her eyes were red. She looked as if she had been crying for hours. I wanted to comfort her, but I didn't know how.

Finally, Jessica spoke. "I feel awful about the way I treated you yesterday. I thought someone from my past was playing a horrible joke on me, but I couldn't deny that you look exactly like I did when I was your age. When I read the legal documents in the manila folder you left, I knew you were the baby I had given birth to. But yesterday when you introduced yourself, I felt as if someone had pulled the ground out from under my feet."

"I didn't mean to upset you," I murmured, exchanging worried, anxious glances with Tyler.

Tyler looked at his watch, slowly rose from his chair and said, "Sarah, if you don't mind, I'd like to go outside for a walk."

I nodded. I knew Tyler wanted me to spend time alone with Jessica.

The instant my husband closed the door behind him, Jessica turned to me and asked, "How did you find me?"

Condensing the details of the struggle I had experienced, I explained the numerous steps I had taken, including the many query letters I had written. But I deliberately neglected to mention that Miss Callie Ann had given me her married name and address.

"My goodness, it sounds as though you went to a lot of trouble and spent a great deal of time to find me," Jessica commented. Then she told me there had been many times when she had been tempted to search for me, but she had not known how or where to begin.

"You thought about me...?"

"Yes, dear, I thought about you often and wondered if you had been adopted by a couple who would give you a good life."

"I had a good life with wonderful parents."

"Are they still living?"

"No, they died many years ago."

"I'm sorry," said Jessica. "Do you have any brothers or sisters?"

"Yes, I have an older brother named Frank, but we're not truly related - he was not adopted."

"But you love him, don't you?"

"Oh, yes, I love Frank. I couldn't love him any more even if we were biologically related to one another. He's a fabulous brother. But because of our age difference – ten years – and the fact he and his wife Linda live so far away, we aren't very close. There are times when I think he has forgotten about me. And I believe I lost him when our parents died. They were the link that held us together. Regardless, I'll always love Frank."

"I'm glad you grew up with a brother," said Jessica.

"Yes, it was nice," I told her, "but I'm curious. Do I have any half-brothers or half-sisters?" (I knew, because Miss Callie Ann had told me that I had a half-sister, but I couldn't let my birth mother know I knew.)

Breaking into my thoughts, Jessica let her voice drop to a whisper and said, "You have a half-sister. My daughter Caroline is twelve and a half years younger than you." Frowning, Jessica added, "But she doesn't know about you."

"Doesn't she have a right to know?"

"She wouldn't understand. If she knew I had had a baby out of wedlock, she'd hate me."

"I believe you're overreacting."

"No, not at all. I never told my husband or my daughter. If I had, and there were times when I was tempted to tell them, they would have lost respect for me. I never told anyone. This is a small town, and if anyone ever found out about my past, my reputation would be ruined. I've kept my secret over fifty years, and I intend to keep it forever."

"That's not fair to me. You're telling me that people who are adopted can't have contact with their biological family because it might embarrass someone?"

133

"I've suffered enough for the terrible mistake I made years ago."

"You consider me a mistake?"

"No, of course not - it has nothing to do with you. But you don't know what I went through before you were born. You have no idea what it felt like to be nauseated every morning for three and a half months. Day in and day out, I had to live with the sorrow and pain I saw in my mother's eyes. I had to listen as she told me over and over again that I had ruined my life. You have no way of knowing what it felt like to watch myself getting bigger and bigger, realizing I didn't have a wedding ring on my finger. You can't imagine how I felt when I had to leave my family and sneak away to a maternity home for unwed mothers, where I was forced to live among strangers for seven months. But the worst part of all was when I delivered my baby and knew I couldn't keep her. My dear, there's no way you could..."

"Oh, but I *do* understand!" I interrupted. "I, too, had a baby out of wedlock and placed her for adoption."

Jessica stared at me in total shock. She hugged me. There was an unspoken bond of savoir-faire between the two of us. For the first time, I felt connected to my birth mother. I felt love, too. It wasn't the sort of love I had had for my adoptive mother, but it was there and it was special.

Leaning forward, Jessica patted my arm, brushed a strand of loose hair from my forehead and said, "Oh, you don't suppose you inherited some terrible trait from me?"

"No, of course not! I have been told a person can't inherit bad traits. She can inherit the color of her eyes, her hair, her skin, her bone structure and perhaps a few behavioral traits, but that's about all."

"I hope you're right."

Because I didn't want to upset Jessica further, I changed the subject and asked her if she would mind telling me what nationality I was. "I've always been curious," I said.

"Well, you're Scotch and Irish. My great-grandparents came from Ireland, and your father's people came from Scotland."

Repeating the words Scotch and Irish, I felt I was discovering my true identity for the first time. Then I asked, as diplomatically as I knew how, "Please, will you tell me something about my birth father?"

Jessica frowned. She took a deep breath, sighed and stared at the floor. "He wasn't the man I thought him to be," she said.

"Is he still alive?"

"No, he died three years ago."

I had never thought much about my birth father, but it was a shock to learn he had died. Now there would always be a piece of the puzzle from my past that would remain missing. Letting my imagination flow freely, I pictured him as a tall, good-looking man, kind and loving in nature. My curiosity concerning him prompted me to ask another question, "Did he come from a good family?"

"Yes, he came from one of the most influential families in the area - a very wealthy, prominent family."

I could see that it was painful for Jessica to talk about my birth father, so to spare her feelings, I changed the subject again.

"I have questions about my birth that only you can answer – little things that most people take for granted," I told her.

Nodding with understanding, she told me what I had weighed at birth and the exact time of day I had been born. She concluded by saying she had had an easy delivery.

"Did you see me? Did you hold me? Did you love me?"

"Yes, I saw you minutes after you were born. Three days later, a nurse brought you into my room and I held you in my arms. I'll never forget how I felt when I looked into your little face. Oh, I loved you so much! I didn't want to give you up, but I did what I thought was best for both of us. I did what I had to do," she whispered, as tears slid steadily down her face.

"Please don't cry. I understand exactly what you must have gone through."

When the silence that followed began to bother me, I asked Jessica if it would be all right if I went outside to smoke a cigarette.

"That won't be necessary, my dear," she said. "You can smoke in here." Reaching under her couch, she pulled out a package of cigarettes, a lighter and an ashtray. "Most of my friends don't know I smoke," she explained sheepishly.

A short time later when Tyler rang the doorbell, he was surprised to see a cigarette in Jessica's hand, but said nothing about it. Instead, he asked her if she would like to join us at a restaurant for lunch.

"Goodness, no!" Jessica answered. "I can't go anywhere with you."

"Why not?" I inquired, staring at her in astonishment.

"Because someone I know might see us."

"What difference would it make?"

"How would I explain you?"

"Well, if someone were to ask," Tyler suggested, "just tell them we're friends of yours from out of town."

"No, I couldn't do that. All my friends know all my other friends. I'm sorry, but I can't go with you."

I was annoyed with my birthmother and believed she was acting paranoid. Yet, knowing she wasn't over the shock of my sudden unannounced appearance on her front doorstep, I didn't argue. I suggested she lie down and rest and asked her if it would be all right if we came back later that evening.

"Yes, that would be nice," she said.

31

Many Questions Answered

On the way back to our motel, I sat quietly, nursing my innermost thoughts. All my life I had had a desperate need to know my birth mother. And now that I had met her, the feeling of contentment went deeper than the sense of sight or touch. I no longer felt suspended in mid-air. At last I knew who I was and where I had come from. It was a wonderful feeling. But I frowned when I thought about Jessica - I wasn't sure how she felt about me. Finally, I said to Frank, "I think my birth mother's secret about having had a baby out of wedlock has eaten at her like a malignant tumor."

"I agree with you," said Tyler. "A secret from the past can destroy a person - it isn't healthy to keep secrets."

"No, it isn't. And there are a couple of other things that bother me."

"Oh?"

"Yes. First of all, I believe I have a right to know my half-sister. When Jessica told me her daughter Caroline doesn't know I exist, it made me angry. Secondly, when I voiced my opinion, Jessica said I had no idea how she had suffered or what she had gone through before I had been born. She made me so angry that I told her about my birth daughter. You know very well I had no intention of telling her about Jennifer."

"Why not?"

"Because I didn't want her to think badly of me."

"Do you think any less of her because she had you?"

"No, of course not. I feel grateful."

"Well, if Jessica is anything like you, and I suspect she is, I'm sure she sympathizes with you."

"I hope she does," I said. Then I yawned. I was exhausted.

After lunch, we returned to our motel room. I stretched out on the bed, looked up at Tyler and whispered, "I'm not going to fall asleep - I'm just going to rest my eyes."

Two hours later when Tyler gently shook my shoulder, I opened my eyes. "Did I fall asleep?"

"Yes, Sarah, and for someone who was just going to rest, you had a long nap."

Twenty minutes later when we returned to Jessica's house, she was sitting on her front porch, obviously waiting for us.

"I've been expecting you," she said warmly. The warmth stayed with her as she escorted us into the living room and we sat down.

Quiet for a moment, I twisted my hair, took a deep breath, swallowed hard and asked the question I had been longing to ask ever since the instant I had met my birth mother: "What should I call you?"

Jessica leaned forward, looked directly into my face and said, "You may call me 'Mother'."

To say I was surprised would be an understatement. I had waited years and years to meet this woman - this stranger - who had just told me I could call her 'Mother', but I couldn't do that. Granted, I had always thought about her as my real mother - that is until I had learned from the search and support group the term birth mother was more appropriate. But whenever the word mother was mentioned, I automatically thought about my adoptive mother - the only mother I had ever known. It had never occurred to me that Jessica would suggest I call her 'Mother'. I was touched. But I didn't know what to say. Most of all, I didn't want to hurt her feelings. For a moment, I was silent. Clearing my throat, I finally said, "Thank you, but perhaps it would be best if I called you Jessica."

"Yes, Jessica will be just fine," she replied.

Relieved that the decision about what to call her was settled, I moved on to another subject. I explained that most people who were adopted worried and wondered about genetic diseases such as diabetes, cancer or Alzheimer's.

"You have nothing to worry about," Jessica assured me. "I'm in good health. The only thing wrong with me is high blood pressure, but with proper diet, exercise and medication, it's under control."

"I'm not worried; I have high blood pressure, too," I told her.

Tyler listened with interest as Jessica and I continued to learn more about one another - like our love for animals and our dislike for wearing shoes. When there was a break in the dialogue, Tyler said, "As long as I've known my wife, she's wanted to find you."

"Yes," I echoed, "I've always been curious. There were many times while I was growing up that my curiosity - and it got worse as I became an adult - affected my day-to-day life. Often when I was in a crowd, I gazed deeply into the women's faces and prayed I'd see a face that resembled mine. I was forever searching for my identity - for you."

"I thought you were happy with your adoptive parents."

"Oh, I was! At least most of the time."

"Then why did you worry so much about finding me?"

"Because I felt connected to you. Besides, whether I was happy or unhappy with my parents had nothing to do with my need to know something about myself: where I had come from and why. Because I was inquisitive doesn't mean I didn't love my parents. However, when I was a child, my mother and I didn't get along well, but I loved her. Unless you're adopted, you can't comprehend how I felt then or how I feel now."

Although Jessica looked puzzled, she said, "Well, I'm glad you loved your mother. I feel indebted to her. She must have been a wonderful woman."

"She was."

Believing it was difficult for Jessica to talk about my mother, I changed the course of the conversation. "You have a lovely home," I said. "Does your daughter help you take care of it?"

"No, but she would if she lived around here."

"Where does she live?"

Ignoring my question, Jessica took a sip of coffee and looked the other way.

Determined to find my half-sister, with or without my birth mother's help, I repeated the question.

As Jessica pondered and drank coffee, stirring it occasionally, she continued to ignore me.

Stubbornly, I waited for an answer.

Finally, Jessica put her coffee cup down and said, "My daughter Caroline and her family - her husband and two daughters - live 250 miles southwest of here."

"Do they visit often?"

"Yes, they come to see me five or six times a year. And at Christmas time," Jessica said, eyes sparkling, "they come to get me so I can spend the holidays with them."

"That's nice. I'm glad you have a daughter you can love."

"I was thrilled when Caroline was born. Over the years, she's been a great comfort to me. However," Jessica said, allowing her voice to drop, "I was terribly disappointed when she decided to marry instead of going away to college. When she and her husband moved away, I was heartbroken."

"Did they have a church wedding?"

"Yes, a large church wedding."

"Where were they married?"

"Right here in the Presbyterian Church. It was a beautiful wedding, but Caroline's father wasn't there to walk down the aisle with her. He had died six months before she was married."

"That's a shame," I sympathized.

Tyler, aware I was questioning Jessica about Caroline so that I could find her, spoke up and said, "Please Jessica, would you reconsider and join us at a restaurant for dinner?"

Jessica's answer was still no. "It's not that I don't want to have dinner with you," she explained. "It's just that I can't take the chance that someone might see us. It has taken me years to put the past behind me and build a good reputation. I'm sorry, but I can't go with you."

I wanted to argue with her, but I didn't. Instead, I kept my thoughts to myself.

The next day, I was melancholy, knowing the time had come to say farewell to Jessica. My heart ached. I felt torn in two different directions. A part of me wanted to stay with her, to get to know her better. But a part of me wanted to rush home to my own world - my familiar surroundings. One thing was clear – meeting my birth mother had been the most rewarding experience of my entire lifetime, an experience more gratifying than I had anticipated, even in my dreams.

Suddenly, a simple fact struck me heavily and painfully, like being hit in the head with a brick. I was the same person I had always been. I was me. Yet knowing my birth mother was a fine, respectable woman who had done what she had to do for both of us, I felt more appreciation, love and respect for my adoptive parents than I had ever felt before. Now I could put their memory to rest, because at last I had my own identity. Most of my questions regarding my background now had answers, and I felt a tremendous surge of relief. Thank God Jessica had not slammed the door in my face.

When we reached Jessica's house, she was waiting for us. With a welcoming smile, she held out her arms and gave me a hug.

Tyler took several Polaroid snapshots of the two of us, even though Jessica fussed about it. "I'm not very photogenic," she complained.

After that, we sat in silence for a few moments, Jessica and I on the couch, Tyler in an armchair.

I asked Jessica if it would be all right if I wrote to her.

"No, " she said. "I would rather you didn't, because if I were to get sick and end up in the hospital, Caroline would surely find your letters. I don't want her to know about you." Pausing, as if in deep agonizing thought, she said, "Perhaps years ago I should have told my daughter that she had a half-sister. But I didn't, and I can't tell her now. So you must not write to me, but you may call me once in awhile."

Again I was disgusted and believed Jessica was acting paranoid. I wanted to tell her Caroline would probably be thrilled to know she had a half-sister. And I wanted to tell her I was determined to find Caroline, but I didn't say anything.

For the most part, I was well pleased with Jessica. There was a charisma about her. I was drawn to her and hoped someday we would become friends.

Reaching over, I put my arms around Jessica. "A big part of me has always loved you," I whispered. Then I kissed her goodbye and thought about what could have been...

32

My Mother is Your Mother?

Although I knew my birth mother was totally opposed to my finding Caroline, and my sense of betrayal almost overwhelmed me, my heartfelt desire to know my half-sister was something I couldn't ignore. I'll always remember Tyler's surprise when I told him I wasn't going home until I had found her.

"Just how do you think you're going to do that?" he asked.

"Oh, it will be easy! All we have to do is find the public library. I'm sure in a town this size there's only one."

We had no trouble locating the library. Excitedly, I walked to the front desk and asked to see the high school year books for the years Caroline would have been in attendance. Having searched for and found both my birth daughter and mother, I considered myself quite an expert in the field of search.

The librarian obliged me with four year books. I took them to a nearby table, sat down and thumbed through them. It wasn't long until I was gazing down at Caroline's high school graduation picture.

"Oh, Tyler!" I said. "She was a beautiful girl! I wonder what she looks like now?"

While Tyler and I admired Caroline's school picture, the librarian, obviously a nosy woman, looked over my shoulder and said, "I know her. My older brother went to school with her."

"Do you know who she married?" I asked.

"No, but I think she married a local boy."

I thanked the librarian, made a photocopy of Caroline's picture and asked for directions to the Presbyterian Church.

"It's two blocks down the street on the lefthand side," she answered.

Thanking her again, Tyler and I made a hasty departure.

Five minutes later, we walked into the Presbyterian Church and found the church office. A woman we assumed to be the church secretary was sitting behind a large desk. When she heard us walking toward her, she looked up. "May I help you?" she asked.

"I'd like to look through your old marriage records," I said.

"Wait here a minute, and I'll go to the storeroom and get them for you."

When the woman returned, she was carrying several large dusty-looking record books. She cleared off a portion of her desk so Tyler and I could sit down and look through them.

Carefully, I turned one page after another and ran my finger slowly down the list of brides' names, written on the righthand side of each page. After going through two and a half record books, I finally found Caroline's name.

"Oh, I found her!" I called out. "Now I know her married name."

The church secretary, an elderly woman who appeared as curious about my inquiries concerning Caroline as the librarian had been, said, "I know her husband's parents."

"Do you know if they still live around here?" asked Tyler.

"Well, her father-in-law died about a year ago, but her mother-in-law still lives here."

"Thanks for your help," I said as I wrote Caroline's married name on a piece of paper and stuck it into my purse. I was thrilled. Finding Caroline's married name had been a lot easier than I had expected, and I stood there trembling with excitement. I felt my heart beating rapidly with anticipation of actually meeting my half-sister.

I grabbed Tyler's arm and literally dragged him out the door, down the front steps of the church and onto the sidewalk. Shielding my eyes from the bright noonday sunlight, I looked up and down the street.

"What are you looking for?" asked Tyler.

"I'm looking for a public telephone booth."

"I saw one outside the library building," he said.

Without a word, I ran down the street, headed toward the telephone. By the time Tyler caught up with me, I was waving a quarter in his face.

"What do you want me to do with this?" he asked, frowning. The question he was afraid to ask was, "What are you up to now?"

"Well, I want you to call Caroline's mother-in-law and tell her you're organizing a class reunion. And tell her you need her son's address and telephone number so you can invite him and his wife to the reunion."

After some effective persuasion from me, Tyler called Caroline's mother-in-law and gave her the class reunion story. The unsuspecting woman willingly gave him the information he had asked for.

"Now we can go home," I said, winking.

That evening when we stopped at a motel, before I did anything else, I picked up the phone and dialed Caroline's number. Originally, I had planned to wait until we returned home to call her, but I was too excited and couldn't put off telling her she and I were half-sisters.

While I impatiently waited for someone to answer the phone, it suddenly dawned on me that I didn't know what I was going to say to her or how I was going to say it. Before I had time to think about it, a woman answered.

"Is Caroline there?" I asked.

"Yes, this is she."

Speaking hurriedly so I wouldn't lose my nerve, I told Caroline who I was and why I was calling. When I finished the lengthy monologue, I was gasping for breath. I listened, but heard nothing.

"Are you there?" I asked.

"Yes, I'm here."

"Well, please say something."

"I can't. I'm speechless."

"I realize you must be stunned," I said. "It isn't every day you get a telephone call like this one, but it's important to both of us. After all, we're half-sisters!"

"What?" she said, surprised.

"We're half-sisters," I repeated.

"You're telling me that my mother is your mother...?"

"Yes!"

"For all I know, you could be a sick, deranged nut."

"I could be, but I'm not," I assured her. "I'll be glad to send you copies of legal documents that will prove who I am." Then I explained I had been searching for my birth mother who was, of course, her mother, for years. I concluded by saying I had recently found her. "I just left your mother's house this morning," I told Caroline.

"Oh, Lord! I can hardly believe what I'm hearing! What was her reaction?"

"She was shocked. But under the circumstances, she had no idea I was coming, and after the initial trauma wore off, I believe she reacted well."

"If you really are my sister, why didn't my mother tell me about you?"

"Because she has always been ashamed of her past. She kept my existence a secret for over fifty years. She didn't want anyone to know she had had a baby out of wedlock. Now your mother believes that if you knew, you would surely hate her."

"She's wrong. I could *never* hate my mother. She should have told me about you a long time ago - that is, if you *are* my sister..."

"I am," I assured her. "But you must remember your mother is from an entirely different generation. She didn't even tell your father."

As if my words were falling on deaf ears, silence followed.

When Caroline finally spoke, she asked if her mother were glad I had found her.

"I think she had mixed emotions." Then I asked Caroline a question. "How do you feel about having a half-sister?"

I need time to let it sink in," she said. "Right now, I'm not sure how I feel."

"You'll feel better after I send you the legal documents."

"Yes, perhaps I will. I need proof," said Caroline.

33

Just Like Sisters

A day and a half later when we drove into our driveway, I turned to Tyler and said, "Home never looked so good."

That night, I slept comfortably in my own bed, and when I awoke the next morning, I felt like a person with a new beginning. No longer did I feel guiilty for having placed Jennifer for adoption. I knew she was all right. I knew she had had a good life. Nor did I feel guilty for searching for and finding my birth mother. Furthermore, I was pleased with the woman I had found. At last I was at peace with myself. What a wonderful feeling!

As promised, I sent Caroline the proof she needed that I was, indeed, her half-sister. She seemed as thrilled about it as I was, and we began corresponding on a regular basis. I invited her and her husband Roger to come for a visit, but she responded that they had already taken their vacation. I was disappointed, but we continued to correspond.

It had been almost a year since I had met my birth daughter Jennifer. Excited, I was looking forward to another visit from her. During the past year she had written numerous friendly letters, had called and sent lovely gifts, a large basket of fruit for Christmas, an expensive "Lladro" cat figurine for my birthday, and for Mother's Day – how wonderful it had been to receive a gift from Jennifer on Mother's Day – a beautiful bouquet of flowers.

I had the opportunity, for the first time since Jennifer's birth, to send her a Christmas present and a birthday present. I wanted to send her presents for every Christmas and every birthday I had missed, but had been warned by members of the search and support group that if I pushed her, I would lose her. But I ignored the warning and kept sending her gifts for any and every occasion I could think of.

Two weeks before Jennifer and her husband were to arrive for their second visit, I received a letter from her that read:

Dear Sarah,

This is probably the most difficult letter I've ever had to write. The last thing I want to do is hurt your feelings.

I enjoyed knowing you were interested in me. I realize you agonized over placing me for adoption. I'm aware of your pain then and now, but I think your decision was wise for both of us. I know, too, that you went to great lengths and expense to find me. But I can't be a part of your life. I have a family here. Although they are not perfect, they are my reality.

You, too, have a family who love you. Tyler is a wonderful man who loves you more than most husbands would, and your daughter Becca adores you. As for me, I must appreciate the family God gave me and care for them.

I want you to know that I will be thinking about you with fondness, but I don't want any further contact. I would appreciate it if you would share my thoughts with Becca.

Fondly, Jennifer

Staring into space, I let the letter slowly drop from my fingertips onto the floor. I was stunned. I was hurt. But most of all, I couldn't figure out what had prompted Jennifer to write such a letter. What had I done wrong, I asked myself? Had I sent her too many gifts? Had I called her too many times? Had I loved her too much? To this day, I don't know why Jennifer, after having been in contact for almost a year, changed her mind and no longer wanted anything to do with me. Perhaps I'll never know. Regardless, I'll always love her as much or more than I did the day she was born. Yet...because I, too, was adopted, a part of me understood that Jennifer's loyalties lay with her adoptive family, and I respected her for that.

Later that evening when I showed Tyler Jennifer's letter, he felt bad.

"One of these days," he said, "when you least expect it, she'll reconsider and get in touch with you."

My answer was, "One of these days, I'll get in touch with her." A little voice deep within me told me all Jennifer needed was time – time to *mature*.

The following spring, I received a letter from Caroline. She suggested we meet in a small town half way between where we lived. I called her immediately and told her I thought it was a wonderful idea. We decided to meet the following weekend.

It took Tyler and me less than two days to make the trip. We arrived Saturday noon and checked into the motel. When we asked the desk clerk if Caroline and her husband had arrived, he said they hadn't.

"We're early," Tyler reminded me.

I found a comfortable chair in the motel lobby and sat down to wait. Nervously, I twisted my hair.

Tyler took our luggage to our motel room.

Lighting one cigarette after another, I wondered if Caroline would ever get there. A few minutes later, I felt someone's hand on my shoulder. Turning abruptly, I saw an attractive woman staring down at me.

"Caroline...?"

"Yes, I'm Caroline. You must be Sarah."

Without hesitation, I stood, put my arms around my half-sister and gave her a hug.

Tyler joined us and introduced himself.

Roger, who had been checking into the motel, walked over, shook hands with Tyler and me, and it wasn't long until the four of us were talking, laughing and having a good time.

I thought Caroline was an extremely pretty young woman. But because of our age difference - almost thirteen years - I felt more like her mother than her sister. And to my surprise, I looked more like her mother than she did. I was disappointed Caroline and I did not resemble one another. Her hair was red. Her eyes were blue. There were no similarities between us that I could see.

Obviously, Caroline noticed the family likeness between Jessica and me.

"Sarah," she said, "I can't get over how much you look like my mother. Why didn't she tell me about you?"

"She had much justification. And more than anything else, she was afraid to tell *you.*"

"If she had," said Caroline, "I would have understood her a lot better. Looking back, I realize she must have thought about you. I remember the many, many times I walked into a room and found her sitting alone, staring into space. When I asked her why she looked so sad, she shrugged and told me she was thinking about the past. But that's all she told me."

"In your mother's generation," I said, "having an illegitimate child was scandalous. But I wouldn't be surprised if she was tempted to tell you, yet she didn't, and then she couldn't."

Caroline nodded. Our visit continued, and after lunch in the motel coffee shop, we found a table by the enclosed swimming pool and sat down.

"Are you planning to tell my mother you and I have met?" asked Caroline.

I couldn't help but notice the emphasis Caroline put on the word "my" when she referred to her mother. Perhaps she wanted a half-sister, but I sensed she did not want to share her mother. Thinking about it, I realized Caroline's reaction was much the same as Becca's had been when Jennifer had suddenly come into her life. Having a half-sister was one thing, but sharing a mother was entirely different. While preoccupied with my thoughts, Caroline repeated her question.

"I haven't decided yet," I answered

"Well, maybe Mother would feel better if she knew the proverbial cat were out of the bag."

147

Roger, a soft-spoken, distinguished-looking man, spoke up then. "I think it would be a mistake to tell her."

"I disagree," said Caroline. "I believe it would be a relief if Mother knew her secret from the past was no longer a secret. But *I* could never be the one to tell her."

As usual, up until now, Tyler had been quietly listening to the conversation. "Why don't you girls concentrate on having a good time together," he said. "You can worry about whether or not you should tell Jessica later."

Caroline and I took Tyler's advice. Our visit continued while the men enjoyed swimming in the heated pool.

The hours passed quickly. Caroline and I talked and talked. We learned many little things about each other. Little things such as our favorite food - steak - and our favorite color - blue.

Reluctantly, I told Caroline about my birth daughter Jennifer. "I'm not proud of my past," I said, "nor am I ashamed of it - Jennifer is a precious girl."

Caroline graciously accepted my account of my past, and I was grateful.

That evening, we found a nice restaurant in town, and the four of us enjoyed delicious steak dinners.

I felt good about having a half-sister. Caroline and I talked and giggled...just like sisters, I thought to myself.

"I was lonesome growing up as an only child," Caroline told me. "It would have been nice to have had an older sister - a sister like you."

"People like me, who are adopted," I responded, "often think about what could have been, but we learn to accept and appreciate the life that was given us."

That evening at the motel, long after our husbands had excused themselves and returned to their rooms to relax and watch television, Caroline and I talked. When we said goodnight, we agreed to meet early the next day for breakfast in the motel coffee shop.

Although I was tired, I couldn't sleep. Meeting my half-sister (I thought of her as a sister) had been an extraordinary experience. I liked Caroline. It was obvious she had had a good life. Jessica undoubtedly had been a wonderful mother. A part of me envied Caroline for having been raised by the woman who had been denied the chance to raise me. Yet I knew I, too, had a good life with my adoptive parents – the only parents I would ever love!

When sleep came, I slept hard. When I awoke the next morning, I looked forward to another visit with Caroline.

Time passed all too quicly as we ate breakfast and talked. After breakfast we went outside, and our husbands took pictures of Caroline and me. Tyler and I took pictures of Caroline and Roger who, in turn, took several of Tyler and me. For a while, we didn't know who was taking pictures of whom. We laughed. We had a good time.

At noon we said our goodbyes.

Caroline hugged me. I hugged her.

148

"Keep in touch," she said as she got into the car with Roger and drove away.

I waved until their car was out of sight.

Tyler turned to me then and asked if I wanted to drive home then or wait to get an early start the next morning.

"I'd rather get an early start in the morning," I told him. "And I was wondering if it would be too far out of our way if we stopped to see Miss Callie Ann."

"Oh, about forty-five or fifty miles," said Tyler. "Why?"

"Because I'd like to meet her. After all, if it hadn't been for her help, I'd probably still be searching for Jessica. Besides, maybe Miss Callie Ann can tell me something about my birth father's side of the family..."

"Sarah, you had this planned!"

"Yes," I confessed. "Before we left home, I called Miss Callie Ann. She's expecting us around lunchtime tomorrow."

34

Rainbow's End

Shortly before noon the next day, Tyler turned off the main highway and headed toward the small town where Miss Callie Ann lived. - the same town Jessica had lived in as a child. About half an hour later, we drove down a peaceful-looking, tree-lined street and found Miss Callie Ann's house.

We got out of the car. I went to the front door and rang the doorbell. A few minutes later, an attractive elderly woman answered the door.

"Oh, my dear," she gasped, staring at me. "You don't have to introduce yourself. You look exactly like your mother, and you resemble your father, too. My goodness, Child! I would have known you anywhere!" Placing her hand to her mouth, she said, "Oh, dear, where are my manners? Please...come in. Lunch is ready." Turning to Tyler, she added, cheerfully, "I hope you're hungry."

While we ate lunch - which was more like a big dinner than a lunch - Miss Callie Ann talked on and on. She told me she had known my birth mother well. Then, pausing, she looked directly into my face and said, "My dear, I hope you didn't tell Jessica you talked with me."

I assured her I had not mentioned her name to Jessica.

"That's good," she said with a long sigh. "If she knew I was the one who told you how to find her, well...I'm certain she would be angry with me."

"Don't worry. It's our secret."

Obviously relieved, Miss Callie Ann told us she had not seen Jessica for many years. "I invited her to our last class reunion, but she was sick and couldn't come. I hope she's all right now."

"She appeared to be just fine."

"Tell me, child - how did she react when you introduced yourself to her as her relinquished daughter?"

"At first she refused to acknowledge me. She was terribly upset, but then......"

"Oh, she'll get over the shock," Miss Callie Ann said, reassuring me. "Just give her time." Then changing the course of the conversation, she asked me about Caroline. "I never met Caroline," she said, "but I've been told she's a fine young woman. Did you like her?"

"Yes, I liked her very much. She's lovely. She's bright and pretty."

"Do you girls look alike?"

"No, we don't look anything alike. It's hard to believe we're related to one another. And I've always wanted a sister, but I realize sisters - even when they have been raised in the same house by the same parents - don't always look alike. Maybe after I send Caroline a few cards with the word 'sister' written on them, I'll feel more like her sister."

"Well," said Miss Callie Ann, "I'm sure it will take awhile to get used to the idea of having a sister."

"I agree with you Miss Callie Ann," said Tyler.

"Oh, please call me Callie. Miss Callie Ann is too long and too formal."

After lunch, Tyler politely excused himself.

I helped Callie clear the table.

Soon we joined Tyler in the formal living room.

Callie asked if we would like to see the town, particularly the house where Jessica had lived as a child growing up.

"Yes, we'd love to," Tyler and I answered in unison.

The three of us got into our car and a few minutes later, following Callie's instructions, pulled in front of a beautiful, stately-looking, two-story stone house. I stared at it, trying to imagine what my birth mother must have been like when she had been a girl living there.

The remainder of the afternoon was spent driving slowly through the beautiful, picturesque old town. Callie pointed out where she and Jessica had attended grade school and high school together. We drove by the corner drug store where, according to Callie, she and Jessica had gone many times to enjoy an ice cream soda.

Callie insisted we stop by the cemetery so she could show me where Jessica's parents and grandparents were buried. Looking back, I feel certain Callie assumed I would sense a certain connection to those who were buried there.

When we got to the cemetery, I shivered all over. I felt like an intruder staring down at the graves of someone else's loved one. I thought about my parents and my grandmother who were buried in a beautiful cemetery far from here. All my life, I had searched for my true identity, and now that I had found my roots, the search had brought me closer to the memory of my adoptive parents. Of course, I was grateful my thirst for knowledge – my curiosity and emotional need to know about myself and my background – had been quenched. I could go on with the rest of my life and put the past behind me. I had reached rainbow's end.

Standing in the middle of the old, well-kept cemetery, I felt I didn't belong. Without a word, I returned quickly to the car. Tears escaped from the corners of my eyes and crept steadily down my face. Oh, how I longed to go home.

When we returned to Callie's house, she took my hand and led me into her bedroom. She tried to pull out the bottom drawer of a large antique dresser, but the drawer was stuck. I tried, too, but it wouldn't budge.

"Tyler, where are you?" I called out. "Tyler, we need you in here."

Tyler appeared in the open doorway.

"Are you girls having problems?" he asked, grimming.

Callie looked up at him, fluttered her eyelashes and smiled.

"Oh, I haven't been called a 'girl' in ever so long," she said. Explaining about the stuck drawer, she told Tyler, "I want to show your wife my old photo albums and my high school year books."

Tyler reached down and pulled out the bottom drawer. "It was warped," he said.

Callie thanked him.

She and I sat down on her bed and looked through the old albums. There were pictures of Jessica when she was a girl, and as a teenager. When we looked through the old high school year books, I learned Jessica had been the president of the glee club and the speech club, and had received many scholastic awards. I was impressed. Suddenly then, I thought about my birth father and asked Callie if she had any pictures of him.

"No," she replied. "He attended a private boys' school in another state."

Disappointed, I asked if she would tell me something about him.

"My dear, you're asking the wrong person. You should have asked your mother."

"I did, but she wouldn't tell me anything about him except that he had died three years ago and had come from a good family who had immigrated to this country from Scotland. I don't even know his first name."

"Well, I can't see any harm in telling you his first name was William. Everyone called him Bill."

"What was his last name?"

"I've already told you more than I should have."

"If you were adopted," I argued, "wouldn't you be curious?"

"Yes, I suppose I would be."

"Can't you at least tell me if I have any half-brothers or half-sisters on my birth father's side of the family?"

Callie hesitated a moment.

It was obvious she was enjoying every minute of the time we were spending together. I suspected she hadn't had this much fun or excitement in her life for years. I also suspected she wanted to tell me everything she knew about my father.

I was right. Callie looked at me and ducked her head like a naughty little girl. Then she said, "You have a half-sister, but she married and moved away. I have no idea where she lives."

"Do I have any half-brothers?"

"Yes, you have a half-brother, too."

"Can you tell me where he lives?"

"Oh, heaven help me, I'd love to tell you, but that information shouldn't come from my lips." Callie put a finger to her mouth, gesturing her lips were sealed forever.

Before I could say another word, Tyler walked into the room.

"Sarah," he said, "are you about ready to leave?"

"Won't you stay for dinner?" Callie coaxed.

"Thank you, but we should be on our way. We want to get an early start in the morning," Tyler responded. He thanked Callie for the delicious lunch and wonderful afternoon.

I was upset. I believed Callie had been on the verge of telling me where my half-brother lived, but now after Tyler's untimely interruption, I thought it would be useless to question her further.

Callie put her arms around me and hugged me.

"Promise you'll stay in touch," she said.

Without an explanation, she disappeared into her kitchen. When she returned, the expression on her face was that of the proverbial cat that had just swallowed the canary. Hugging me again, she said, "Oh, I wouldn't have missed meeting you for anything in the world. I can't remember when I've had a better time."

Callie accompanied us to the car.

After I got into the car and buckled my safety belt, she reached in through the open window and gently kissed my cheek.

I smiled and thanked her for the delightful day we had spent together.

Tyler put the key into the ignition and we were about to drive away when Callie shoved a small piece of paper into the palm of my hand and folded my fingers over it.

"Don't you tell a living soul where you got this," she whispered.

As soon as we were out of Callie's sight, I unfolded the piece of paper and found she had given me my half-brother's name, address and telephone number.

By the time we checked into a motel and finished getting ready for bed, I had decided to telephone Bill.

When I told Tyler my decision, he smiled and said, "Well, Sarah, as long as we're in this area, you might as well meet all your biological relatives."

I squeezed Tyler's hand and thanked him for his understanding.

"Oh, you've been great!" I said. "No one in the world could have been more supportive."

Moments later when I placed the long-distance call, a woman answered. I asked if I could speak to her husband.

"I'm sorry," said the woman, "but Bill isn't here. I'm his wife Ellen. May I help you?"

"Yes, perhaps you can," I said. Then I explained that I had been told by a reliable source that her husband was my half-brother.

"I wouldn't be a bit surprised."

I was puzzled by her reply. She didn't argue. She didn't tell me that I had been given the wrong information. I suspected then and still do today that Callie had telephoned her and told her I would be getting in touch with Bill. That's the only logical explanation for Ellen's lack of surprise in response to my call.

Before our conversation ended, Ellen told me that she understood my need to know something about myself.

"If I were adopted," she said, "I would be curious, too."

When I hung up the phone, the more I thought about it the more I was convinced that Ellen's nonchalant attitude stemmed from having been warned I would be calling her husband.

When Tyler asked if I had told Ellen that I planned to pay them a visit, I shook my head.

"No, I didn't tell her, because I was afraid she would say no, don't come."

The next morning, Tyler and I were on our way again. This time to meet Bill.

I watched for road signs that would lead us to our destination. We had driven less than an hour when I spotted the sign we had been looking for. We turned off the main highway and drove down a bumpy gravel road. About an hour later, we were driving down the main street of the smallest town I had ever seen in my life.

"They call this a *town*?" I mouthed as I glanced out the car window. There was a gas station, a grocery store, a funeral home, a post office and a sheriff's office. That was all there was to see.

"It's a typical small western town," said Tyler as he parked in front of the sheriff's office. He was about to get out when I noticed a "closed" sign in the window.

I got out of the car and looked up and down the deserted street. The town looked like a ghost town. Then I saw a woman coming out of the grocery store. I ran up to her and asked if she knew where Bill's ranch was located.

"Yes, everyone knows where Mr. Bill lives," she answered.

Tyler joined us and asked the woman for directions.

"You have to go back to the main highway," she said. "After six or seven miles, you will come to an intersection. Take a right and drive about ten miles farther until you see a high wooden fence. The fence goes on and on for miles," she said with a wide gesture. "Keep going, and after you've driven about eight miles, you'll see the entrance to Mr. Bill's ranch. The house is about a mile off the road."

We thanked the woman and got back into our car.

We followed her directions carefully, and it wasn't long until we found the entrance to the ranch. We turned and drove down a long winding driveway that led to Bill's house.

Tyler stopped the car.

I sat there and didn't move. I just stared at the beautiful, rambling ranch house.

"Sarah, aren't you going to get out of the car?" asked Tyler.

"I don't know. I'm sick of introducing myself to strangers I'm related to who don't even know I exist. Now that we're here, I'm not too sure it was a good idea. After all, I don't have any proof that Bill is my half-brother."

"We're here, Sarah. You should meet him. If you don't, you will always be curious about your birth father's side of your birth family."

I trembled inwardly as we walked to the front door and rang the bell.

The woman who answered introduced herself as Bill's wife, Ellen.

"I've been expecting you," she said. "Won't you please come in? My husband is eager to meet you."

I sat nervously on the edge of a chair. The formal living room where we were sitting was furnished with expensive-looking antiques. The furnishings reminded me of the house where I had grown up. I thought lovingly about my adoptive parents.

Then a man walked into the room. He was tall and thin. His hair was dark, his eyes hazel. The little mustache he wore gave him a look of distinction. Immediately I thought that he looked like me.

The man stared at me.

I stared back at him.

"My wife tells me you are my half-sister," he said, continuing to stare at me.

"Well, that's what I have been told."

"You probably *are* my half-sister, but don't expect me to feel any instant love for you."

I was tired, emotionally worn to a frazzle. My nerves were almost to the breaking point. What this man said and the way he said it made me angry. My temper flared.

"I don't expect a damn thing from you. The last thing I need is another brother. I already have a brother whom I love."

"I didn't mean to upset you," said Bill. "It isn't every day that a person comes along and tells me she's my half-sister."

"You will have to excuse my wife," Tyler interjected. "She's been through a lot lately."

Bill's wife stood then and announced that she had an important errand to run.

I suspected she wanted to get out of the room and away from what could turn into an ugly confrontation. Yet I kept my suspicions to myself. A big part of me regretted having come here, and I wished I could get up and leave. I wanted to go back to the safety of my own life with people I loved and felt comfortable with.

The instant Ellen walked out the front door, Bill held out his arms to me.

"Sarah," he said, "come over here and give me a hug."

Involuntary tears crept down my face. I couldn't understand the sudden change in Bill's attitude toward me. Like a child given explicit instructions, I obeyed and rose from my chair.

Bill moved toward me, and when we were face to face, he hugged me. His arms felt strong. For a moment, I felt a bond of love between the two of us.

"My wife," said Bill almost apologetically, "will never, ever accept you as part of our family."

"I don't want to be a part of your family," I whispered. "All I want is to find out something about my birth father. What sort of man he was and..."

"I understand exactly how you must feel," said Bill. "I'll be glad to tell you about him."

Bill and I sat on the Queen Anne sofa and faced one another. He told me about the man who had been my birth father. I was relieved to know I had nothing to worry about regarding any genetic diseases other than high blood pressure. My birth father, according to Bill, was a good man. A man who had provided well for his family. A man of integrity who had been respected in the community. An honest, reliable man who had given large amounts of money as well as time to church and charity.

"I was about fourteen years old," said Bill, "when the gossip about my father and a young woman - your birth mother - swept through our small town. I suppose in his youth he was a ladies' man. But my mother, a wonderful, strong woman, loved him. Although she must have been terribly hurt to learn that her husband had fathered another woman's baby, she undoubtedly loved him enough to fogive him. Besides, divorce was unheard of in those days."

"You mean you've always known you had a half-sister?"

"Yes, I've always known. But I never dreamed I would meet her."

"I know you have a sister. Does she know about me?"

"No, and you must promise that you will never, ever try to find her. Lillian is a sensitive, high-strung young woman who adored her father. It would ruin her life if she knew about you. She's a person who lets everything bother her, and she never gets over it. It would break her heart, and it would destroy her if she learned her beloved father was your father, too."

"Don't worry, I won't try to find her. I know how she feels. I had a wonderful father whom I adored. Most daughters adore their fathers and put them on a pedestal, you know..."

Tyler interrupted me by clearing his throat and looking at his watch. I knew he was telling me it was time for us to leave.

There was a long moment of silence as Bill looked into my face, studying me. Then he escorted us to the front door and walked with us to our car. He leaned down and hugged me. I hugged him and thanked him for the information about my birth father.

Bill smiled and put his arms around me again and held me close. He spoke softly, "Sarah, go home and get on with your life. Put the past behind you." Pausing, he added, "I would have loved having you as a sister."

As we drove away, I waved goodbye to my half-brother. I knew I would never see Bill again. I also knew I would never forget him.

My search was over.

For awhile, I sent my birth mother gifts for her birthday, Mother's Day, Christmas and Easter. I called her often.

Five and a half years have gone by. Jessica has never gotten in touch with me. I have quit sending gifts. I have quit calling her. It is obvious that she does not want me in her life. But I can accept this. Although I liked the woman I found, just finding her made me appreciate the memory of my adoptive mother even more. I shall forever be grateful to Jessica for giving me life. I am sorry I upset her by going behind her back and finding her daughter, my half-sister Caroline, something Jessica begged me not to do. I am sorry if I caused her any pain or sleepless nights. There is no doubt in my mind that when Jessica dies - a *long* time from now, I hope - she will go to Heaven. When she does, she will meet my adoptive mother there - the only mother I ever knew and loved.

Caroline and I have continued to correspond. I am glad I met her. I am glad we are friends.

It is difficult for me to accept that my birth daughter Jennifer has chosen not to be a part of my life. Perhaps in many ways she is wiser than I am. I will always love her and think of her. Deep in my heart, she will always be my baby, even though I relinquished her to be raised as someone else's daughter. I'm thankful to know she is alive.

Becca and I have become closer than we were before the search. I appreciate the baby God gave me to love - my beautiful Becca.

Frank is as important to me today as he was when I was the little girl who followed him everywhere. No one could have a brother she loves more than I love Frank.

Tyler and I still enjoy attending the monthly meetings of the search and support group. The last meeting we attended, one of the women, still searching for her birth mother, asked me if I would go through the search and reunions if I had known at the beginning what I know now.

"Oh, yes, I would!" I exclaimed. "Although the search for my birth daughter and mother seemed endless, took a toll on my health, put a strain on my marriage and, at times monopolized my life, it was well worth all the stress, aggravation and expense. There were times, however, when I wondered if I would survive. The reunions were more melodramatic than I had dreamed possible. Many other people's lives were affected, too. But after I found my biological family ties, I felt whole for the first time in my life. I experienced an inner contentment that brought with it peace.

"Yes, with God's help, the love and support from my husband Tyler and my daughter Becca, assistance from Joan Banner and encouragement from the members of this group, I'd do it all over again.

"I went chasing rainbows and, like Dorothy, was granted an audience with the Wizard of Oz."

Laurel Lynn, author of **Chasing Rainbows**, has a unique understanding of the adoption triangle – birthparents, adoptees, and adoptive parents. She grew up as an adopted daughter, curious about her biological families ties. When she became a young woman, she, too, gave up a daughter for adoption. Her birth daughter and husband adopted two girls, thus making them three generations of adopted girls.

She has been published in several magazines. She is a mother and grandmother and lives in Olathe, Kansas, with her husband, Don. Now that she is no longer *Chasing Rainbows*, she is free to go on to her next dream – writing children's stories and some day a novel.